Moon Child

Growing Up NASA

Author – Betty Byrnes

Betty Byrnes

Copyright © 2012 Betty Byrnes

All rights reserved. No part of this publication may be reproduced or transmitted, in any form or by any means, electronic, mechanical, photocopying, recording, or otherwise, or stored in any retrieval system of any nature without written permission of the copyright holder and publisher, application for which must be made to the publisher.

DEDICATION

To my beautiful children and grandchildren,
each and every one of you:
Justin, Melissa, Shannon,
Loren Jr., Katrina,
Charlie, Kale, Loren, Morgan, Tayler,
Fiona, Logan and Trinity.

I dedicate this book with all
my love and prayers
for a life well lived, full of
happiness and joy.
Strive always to be all that
God created you to be.

*"May the road rise up to meet you, may the wind be
ever at your back.
May the sun shine warm upon your face and the rain
fall softly on your fields.
And until we meet again, May God hold you in the
hollow of his hand."*

~ Old Irish Blessing

CONTENTS

	Acknowledgments	i
	Introduction	iii
PART 1	Lancaster Land of the High Desert Edwards	1
Chapter 1	The Family – Ave J-6	3
Chapter 2	From Whence We Came	9
Chapter 3	The Cloverleaf Rug	20
Chapter 4	Brother – Dennis	26
Chapter 5	Sister – Patty	30
Chapter 6	The Bicycle	33
Chapter 7	The Accident	39
Chapter 8	The Announcement	44
PART 2	Virginia Land of Forest and Beaches Langley	47
Chapter 1	Hampton, Virginia	49
Chapter 2	Henry Street	58
Chapter 3	Buckroe Beach	69
Chapter 4	STG Brings Big Changes	76
PART 3	Houston – Land of Rodeos and Astronauts NASA	87
Chapter 1	Houston, Texas	89
Chapter 2	Glen Valley Avenue	98
Chapter 3	Ginger	109
Chapter 4	Kennedy Space Speech	115
Chapter 5	Out At Sea On Carriers	123
Chapter 6	The Reality Of Fear	133

Chapter 7	Malt Shops and Fast Food	138
Chapter 8	Bullets Change Everything	142
Chapter 9	Six For Six	149

PART 4	California	157
	Back To Where We Started	
	Aerospace	

Chapter 1	Los Angeles	159
Chapter 2	Hanna and Etough Streets	165
Chapter 3	Moorcroft Street	179

PART 5	California	189
	Retirement	
	NASA	

Chapter 1	Back In The Game	191
Chapter 2	Things Change Quickly	195
Chapter 3	Promise Fulfilled	203
Chapter 4	Mom's Last Gift	212
	Oh Danny Boy	217

| PART 6 | Conclusion | 219 |
| | Everything Comes Full Circle | |

	Journal Notes	221
	Introduction Memoirs	233
	Dad's Memoirs	235

Betty Byrnes

HEARTFELT ACKNOWLEDGMENTS

There is no greater agony than bearing an untold story inside you. ~ Maya Angelou

First and foremost thank you to God for allowing me the privilege of growing up in the Byrnes family and appointing me the assignment of documenting my minuscule everyday life in a way that honors my most special parents and family heritage.

Thank you to mom and dad for your never failing, endearing, stalwart love for our family. I will always LOVE you both. "Dad... mission complete."

Thank you to my son, Justin Stahl, for his never ending love, respect and loyalty. I could not ask for a better or more loving son. I pray that you and all my children and grandchildren, whom I love so deeply, will take this book as an inspiration for all God has created you to be. Know deep in your minds, souls and hearts you come from greatness and brilliance. Hold tight to the fact that God has a special personal plan for each of you. May your grandfather's legacy and example open your eyes and hearts to great possibilities in your lives. That by his example you will see when you are called according to God's purpose and when you work hard you can reach for the stars... and dreams do become reality.

Thank you to Dr. Thomas Fera and Junko Nagashima for your educated encouragement and insightfulness which continued to spur me onward in the completion of this book.

My heartfelt deep thanks go out to my dear friend, Susan Brookes, whose continual, anxious, uplifting push to read each new chapter motivated me to bring this book to fruition. You have been a never ending source of encouragement. Thank you, Susan, for your contagious interest, superior excitement, love and support.

Thank you to Robyn Starkand my compadre in adventure whose encouragement and interest in this project gave me the energy, fortitude and single mindedness to move forward.

Also a sincere thank you to Mimi O'Garren whose brilliant, artistic creation brought my vision for the cover of this book alive. You so clearly understood what was in my mind and heart.

Deep gratitude also to Jan Carlson, whose patience, kindness and generosity of spirit made this book a reality with her superior skill at editing.

Lastly deepest gratitude, thanks and acknowledgement to Michael Jackson, an amazing man with a golden heart and bottomless spirit of giving, for without your inspiration to excellence, art and your enduring global encouragement for every person to reach for the stars and moon, I'd never have known the ability to write a meaningful story lay within me. In your death and great loss my life was forever changed and this documentation given birth.

Introduction

Moon Child: Growing Up NASA is a labor of love and my attempt at the completion of unfinished memoirs for my father. This candid account of a simpler time where extraordinary events took place was originally meant as a personal recording of our generational family legacy. I felt God called me to write this book for my children and grandchildren as a way to mark in time the efforts of their grandfather and/or great grandfather, an instrument of light to point the way to their own personal greatness and calling in life and to learn on a personal level their incredible family history along with the small family stories of living life in a different simpler era. May this book inspire each of them, no matter what path or plan God has for them, to be God's Glow. If you are born to fly to space or to wait on tables you are of service in God's plan. Do it with unaffected love and service in your heart and you will be God's Glow.

To the reader if you are looking for detailed descriptions of NASA flights and research this is not the book for you. This is a recollection of fond and sometimes painful memories growing up in a NASA home during the post-war era of WWII and the Space Race, the Baby Boomer age. This book conveys the everyday story of a little girl growing up in the 1950s, the youngest of three children in a National Advisory Committee for Aeronautics (NACA) and National Aeronautics and Space Administration (NASA) family. It is a simple, true life story of a little girl and her adoring love of her Daddy and their everyday family experiences during the most adventurous and historic time in modern history.

God first gave me a kernel of a thought, a recollection of a precious childhood experience. It was a niggling memory that kept recurring which gave way to a tsunami of lifetime memories and the birth of this book:

"Sandwiched between horses and marching bands we were slowly driven down the city streets of Houston with cheering crowds rubber necking, gaping back at us. I gazed up at high rise buildings dwarfing us while seated in the convertible back seat with my family, my blonde hair peeking out from under my turquoise cowboy hat following dad's direction to wave and smile big at the crowd just like a little junior Miss America. The wave and smile came naturally for dad, his big jovial smile lighting up the crowd as he humbly waved back, saying hello, many people wanting to shake his hand. He was humble, took it all in stride, shaking his head in disbelief with his typical rolling laugh. He knew they were not really there for him but for NASA and the astronauts. They were the real stars, he was their representative. He had been to Houston many times paving the way, meeting the mayor and city officials working out the details to move NASA to Houston, helping to create NASA's main headquarters as the country embarked on the "Final Frontier". The parade route ended, we disembarked the open convertible car and entered the giant stadium for the rodeo, my first ever western, cowboy rodeo. The unequivocal and distinct excitement in the air was enthralling and hypnotizing. Our little family moved forward, walking together, hand in hand with dad at the lead along with the crushing flow of the crowd."

This is my first book. I am not a professional author or writer. I am a mother and a grandmother, a sober alcoholic of 34 years at this time in 2014, one day at a time. Unlike my brilliant father my life has been a series of lessons in survival. Yet I am more than just a survivor I am a victor in life. I have been married and divorced 3 times. I jokingly admit that it's not as many as Elizabeth Taylor (my children are my diamonds)... but enough to make my mark in the world.

From the start, I felt God was guiding me to write this book, an assignment from God not only to relay this story as family legacy but as an eye opener for me to 'own' my wonderful childhood. I could never have imagined the blessing of freedom and uplifting joy God had in store for me as page after page released me from a lifetime of pain and revealed my true, nurturing and joyful childhood. If you enjoy reading my story or it helps you in anyway then that is even more of a blessing.

Gratefully, I am the survivor of alcoholism, drug addiction, sexual and spousal abuse and all the delusional paradigms of shifting blame that come with addiction of any sort. I no longer carry shame and long ago learned it's easy to blame your parents and others around you as the source of your own misery, mistakes, poor choices and unhappiness. For me, the writing of Moon Child was the final catalyst in discovering the microscopic honesty required to open the door to crystal-clear forgiveness, to recognize patterns in my life and the true reality of my beautiful childhood.

In the future, another book about the darker side of my life and ultimately overcoming abuse and shame may perhaps be penned; however for now this cathartic journey for me has been a spiritual, healing process I would not trade for the world.

Much laughter and many tears flowed, as I discovered a deep newfound compassion for my parents. While writing this diary of Byrnes family legacy God blessed me with a fresh, clear-eyed retrospective. God walked me through each step of this pilgrimage into my past, filling my heart with gratitude as an avalanche of recollections poured forth. Via the writing of this book, God shined His brilliant healing light on my life and deeply edified my love for my family and parents.

Please join me on my journey
as I share my life ...

Moon Child: Growing Up NASA.

Moon Child: Growing Up NASA

Moon Child: Growing Up NASA

Part 1
Lancaster
Land of High Desert
Edwards

I love my father as the stars — he's a bright shining example and a happy twinkling in my heart.

~Terri Guillemets

Betty Byrnes

Chapter 1

The Family – Ave J-6

It was late afternoon, the air was crisp and clear. Chattering away, happily playing in the front yard with mommy inside cooking dinner, the sweet little towhead blonde caught site of her father who after a long days work at the local Air Force Base had just pulled his 1954 Buick into the driveway. Her little voice rang out in glee, "Daddy, Daddy!" as she glimpsed her hero, her beloved. Quickly forgetting her toy with complete abandon she shot down the drive way.

"Daddy! Daddy, Pick me up! Throw me up!"

She catapulted herself into the air with absolute certainty that her daddy would be there to catch her. His blue eyes sparkled as a big beautiful smile spread across his face. His deep jovial laugh filled her with such warmth and love as he swooped her up in his strong arms and tossed her lovingly higher and higher into the air, catching her firmly each time.

"There you go, Betty Bean. How's my 'Little Bit' today?" She felt as though she was flying. "Higher, Daddy, higher!"

This was his loving greeting on this day like many other days from his sweet little girl. I loved these greetings, these hugs and kisses. This was my early life as the youngest daughter of Martin Aloysius Byrnes, Jr.

We lived in a quiet neighborhood in the high desert known as Antelope Valley, in a small town named Lancaster, California. Dad jokingly referred to all who lived here as "desert rats." Lancaster was a dusty, desert community of pilots and government employees which lay on the outskirts of the Mojave desert not a far drive from Edwards Air Force Base, also known at the time as Edwards High Speed Flight Station. To the South a short drive away was Ames Research Center, Moffett Field, California. It was in 1946 that dad received his first assignment to NACA as 'Procurement Clerk' landing him and mom in this desert dust bowl. It wasn't long before Lancaster naturally became the perfectly centered roosting spot for families of test pilots and the NACA space research team.

Our Lancaster street was a generic Avenue J-6 filled with typical 1950's square shaped, cookie cutter, suburban neighborhood homes which sprung up across the country after the war. Each home had a nice size yard, redwood fenced backyard and a large shade tree in the front yard. Homeowners were free to paint their homes any color; dad painted ours forest green with white trim.

Next door, the Scott Crossfield family lived in a white house with the same big Elm tree in the front yard as ours. He was a test pilot who flew the X-15. Down the street lived the family of Jim McKay the twin brother of John "Jack" McKay, another test pilot who flew the X-15. Jim had lost part of his arm as a child while playing with cherry bomb fireworks. Around the corner was the Day family whose father also worked on base. Their oldest son was a beatnik and played the bongos. Even at the early age of four I thought he was mysterious and just the coolest ever. Around another corner on the other side were the Franklins whose dad also worked on the base. Their son, David, and my brother, Dennis, became a mischievous duo. Behind us on both sides were also others who worked on base for NACA, the Rogers and the Gigax families.

Together they were a lively, gregarious, close knit group of people. It was a happy, loving neighborhood where parties, barbecues and get-togethers happened daily, or at least, weekly.

The dad's had rigged the backyard redwood fence so that the gate just at the meeting point where all four yards connected spun like a revolving door. We could go from one house to the other without ever leaving our backyards. All the kids streamed back and forth to play with the swing set, slide, teeter-totter, see-saw, hula hoops, toys and sandbox. Many happy hours were spent playing here while mom hung the clothes on the clothesline after washing them by hand with the aid of the wringer washing machine.

We felt safe and loved. I remember the familiar smell of freshly percolated coffee and scrumptious, fresh baked goods shared in early morning coffee klatches. There the warmth of the early morning sun hit the kitchen windows making the red and white gingham or Swiss Dot Priscilla curtains glow, depending on which kitchen we gathered in. All the wives would be talking and laughing while the children played close by or out in the backyards.

For a time we had a cute, fun, rambunctious, little, white dog to wrestle with in the backyard until mom's newly-hung, flapping sheets on the clothesline became his entertainment. Two sessions of scrubbing and mending grass-stained sheets with the Singer sewing machine and he was deemed history, earning him a trip to the pound. I cried crocodile tears when the big white, dog-catcher truck arrived to seize him. I begged mom to allow him to stay but she was adamant and that was that. He was gone for good leaving a hole in my heart. Practicality took precedence.

Dad dove into a furniture and wood-working class for adults at the local elementary school which resulted in some very cool furniture. He crafted a thick, wood-slab, rectangular, '50s style coffee and end tables with cool, black wrought iron legs, three geese in flight, twin size bed frames for the children, a picnic table, and eventually, the sand box in the back yard.

Our backyard was the prime children's play area for the four revolving gate homes. The dad's erected a big swing set during a neighborhood barbecue near the sand box where many wondrous, skillful feats were displayed. Swing set stardom and jungle gymnastics were readily performed for the parents as we hung off bars and jumped great heights from high-flying swings, landing on the thick St. Augustine grass. They would always clap and cheer for us as they enjoyed their beer and grilled hamburgers and hot dogs. Hoola Hoops also provided great entertainment for the children. I became very proficient at hoola hooping, so much so that the adults would inevitably... and hilariously... be inspired to try their hand at it.

Eventually mom discovered that dad's sand box was a big draw for the neighborhood cats at night, who had turned it into a giant kitty litter box. So, it was emptied and declared off limits. There was so much else to keep us busy; we never missed it.

Special treats and fresh bread could be purchased from the Helm's Bakery Truck, which drove through the neighborhood daily, much like ice cream trucks today. The Helms truck brought bread and the Good Humor truck brought ice cream. When the whistle blew on the Helm's truck, we'd all come running. The kids with change in our little mitts for sweet delectables and the moms to buy snacks and the weekly supply of bread, which would then be stored in vented bread boxes with Bakelite handles. The truck would stop, the back doors would be opened by the very official Helms man dressed in his white uniform and hat, which always reminded me of a skipper onboard ship. He'd roll open the drawers and shelves loaded with a plethora of cupcakes, cookies, sweet rolls and breads. The smell of freshly-baked bread and cookies greeted our noses. The cupcakes and cookies were just at my eye level, inviting little hands to reach out for them. I quickly learned the abrupt Helms Man's rule as he'd bark, "You touch it. You buy it."

When we heard the whistle we needed to decide quickly what we wanted because the Helms Man had a schedule and did not like indecision or children hanging around his truck. In spite of his curtness, we could never resist the sweetness held within the Helms truck and inevitably washed it down with cold fresh milk from glass bottles the Milk Man left at the front door every few days in exchange for our empty bottles.

In first grade our class took a field trip to the dairy farm where the same fresh milk was produced by many cows in green pastures. We learned the process of bringing the cows in to be lined up in their stalls for milking by the machines which were attached to their udders. Then those same sterilized glass bottles that were delivered to our front door were refilled with fresh homogenized milk for more daily deliveries. This was true recycling long before it became fashionable or politically correct.

My brother two years older than me was a rough and tumble kid who knew his way around the block. I was a little fire house on wheels, always fighting to keep up with my big brother and sister, as well as the other kids on the block, and became quite a daredevil. I was a painfully shy child but when push came to shove, I was always in the mix. This feisty temperament did not hold me in good graces with the Camp Fire Girls, where on a field trip not wanting to be left behind and true to the neighborhood rules of engagement, I fought to be in the front. The leader called my mother and requested I leave the troop as I wasn't demure enough to fit in. My response to mom was, "I don't like their stupid troop anyway." For years I proudly held on to the claim that I was eighty-six'ed from the Camp Fire Girls at the age of five never to be pigeon holed, proving from the gate the rebellious streak in me prevailed and groups and cliques were not to my liking. I was then and still am forever marching to my own drummer.

There were three of us, towhead blondes with light blue green eyes, little stair steps when all lined up. It was the end of the WWII era and the beginning of the '50s and having just returned from the service, my parents did their best to supply their portion of children to the '50s postwar baby boom.

Chapter 2

From Whence We Came

As if randomly dropped in the middle of the desert, our clutch of a housing development ran alongside a stretch of vacant desert filled with tumble weeds, scrub brush and sand. One side of the fence was my green oasis called home and the other side a daunting, endless no man's land that called for an adventuresome soul like mine. I remember so vividly several times on Saturday mornings after cartoons being scooped up and carried by my father in his strong arms out to this field. He would hold me, my sister clinging to his pant leg and my brother standing close and would point up saying, "Look! Look up in the sky! Scott will fly by!" Then as we raised our little chins, tilted back our heads, mouths gaping open, looking up at the brilliant blue California sky the most powerful, magnificent, black, fighter jet would whooosh by over head.

Flying over the houses Scott Crossfield would look down at us smiling, wave from the cockpit window and gently rock the jet back and forth, making the wings seemingly wave hello. We'd all wave back yelling, "Hello!" I could hear cheering from the backyards. The jet would make another roaring pass, shaking everything around us with its powerful jet noise. Dad would look at me in his arms, then back at the jet while waving to the pilot and laugh that jovial belly laugh that so easily rolled out of him. The sound of my dad's cascading laugh never failed to engulf me in a blanket of warm love.

Playing inside or out the loud sound of a sonic boom as jets broke the sound barrier were a regular occurrence in our lives and always brought an assuring feeling that dad and his friends were at work close by. Ultimately and most loudly the Shuttle's re-entry 'boom' would become a familiar welcome sound as well. Sonic booms were our friends... a signal that everything was ok, pilots were at work and play in the air and astronauts were home safely.

Both my parents served in the United States Army during WWII. My dad, a handsome, brilliant Captain in The Army Corp of Combat Engineers, trained in 1942 at Riddle Aeronautical Institute, Dorr Field in Arcadia, Florida at the Southeast Army Air Forces Training Center. During WWII he served his country as a military engineer, bravely working to construct temporary runways, airplane landing strips and bridges in the South Pacific, Japan and Europe. I remember him sharing what seemed in retrospect to be fun, interesting stories of uncomfortable rides in Army jeeps on back Island roads, praying to God that they would get the job done for incoming troops and get home safely.

My mother, Kathleen Rita Curran (Katie for short) a Lieutenant WAC (Women's Army Corp) in The Army Nurse Corps served as an Army nurse on board carrier ships in the Atlantic Ocean and in military hospitals in France. Never the type to primp in front of a mirror, she was trim and fit, a no-frills woman. Her brown, tight curls framed her square shaped, bright, clear skinned face and her rosy cheeks set off her hazel green eyes. When she smiled her whole face lit up, spotlighting an endearing small gap she very much disliked between her two front teeth. Never considering herself to be a pretty woman, she was the opposite of vain, opting for a down-to-earth, tomboy approach to life. She was a spunky, energetic, sportswoman-type with a fun sense of humor and a zest for life who excelled at basketball and ice skating as a child and bowling as an adult.

She expressed she absolutely hated the journey across the Atlantic on board the military Hospital Ships. In disdain, she spoke only of being sea sick most of the time on board ships and affirmed this by vowing to never take another boat ride. It didn't help that she had never learned to swim. As a result of this fear of water and the ocean, she forced herself to take swimming lessons, learning to swim with me at the age of five. I remember speaking words of encouragement to her in the pool and seeing her elated smile as she learned she could float, tread water and swim right alongside me.

She remained reticent her entire life, keeping her war time nursing experiences private. She was deeply family-oriented, sending most of her military pay home to support her mother and family in upstate New York as her father, my grandfather, had passed away not long before she had finished nursing school.

Marty and Katie, my parents, both deeply loved their country, church and God. Their love for one another stood the test of time. God first brought them together in Marseille, France while on leave; where they were introduced by friends on a blind date. It was truly love at first sight. My father would walk or hitch a ride traveling up to 50 miles to see mom on base in her barracks. They fell head over heels for one another, passionately courting while stationed in France, dating and breathing in the French country side.

Later in life, I learned my mother's fellow WAC sisters kept guard as look outs at the front doors of the corrugated, tin-can type Quonset Hut they called the barracks. These portable huts served as Army based housing for the troops during WWII. Mom shared later in life that they were miserable places, sweltering in the summer and freezing in the winter. On dad's visits, he crawled in the side window for a private rendezvous and the ladies outside would whistle a warning if anyone was coming so dad could make his get away by sneaking back out the window.

WWII victoriously ended and both separately returned home; however their love was strong and in no time they reunited in the states.

At his family's urging, my father had studied to be a Jesuit priest before the war. He attended and graduated from the Maryland Seminary, Marymount University in 1938. Much to his family's chagrin, he had been bitten with the bug to fly at a very early age. His fascination with the Wright Bothers, Kitty Hawk and airplanes was fueled with the outbreak of war, pulling him toward the military and igniting dreams of becoming a pilot. His dreams were dashed when he washed out of flight school; although his love of airplanes and flight were never extinguished.

My father chose to follow his love of airplanes in what he called "the airplane business" and with my mother's support and love, he abandoned his family's plans to become a priest and a whirlwind stateside courtship ensued. They traveled to both the Catskills, in upstate New York and Hampton, Virginia, where they broke the news of their engagement, introducing their future spouses to their prospective families. They quietly slipped off to marry in a small, intimate Maryland, Catholic church with only their best friends and the priest present. The priest, a fellow seminarian and good friend of dad's.

Mom's maid-of-honor, Mary Martin, was a fellow WAC and dear friend. The close bond which developed while enlisted remained their entire lives and ultimately, Mary honored my mother and father by naming her daughter, Katie and giving her son the middle name Marty after my father. I have also kept the generational friendship moving along, developing a wonderful friendship with Mary's lovely daughter, Katie.

Buoyed on to follow his dream of air flight in any way possible, the government's first assignment for dad removed them from their parent's and family on the green, east coast and planted them in the parched, west coast desert. The new assignment: National Advisory Committee for Aeronautics (NACA), Edwards Air Force Base, Mojave, California. At Edwards, dad worked with other brilliant engineers and pilots on the "X" aircraft ventures, reaching for higher and higher supersonic speeds and heights culminating in X-15 supersonic flight. This assignment, this quest would eventually catapult man into space to orbit around the Earth and ultimate space travel. It has been written that some of the most "far out" aeronautical engineers worked for NACA in the early 1950's and my dad was one of them.

This move to the West coast was a drastically big move in those days as traveling this distance across country meant they would rarely ever see or speak to their families as all communication was mainly done by letter. Long distance phone calls were not an everyday luxury. The average person did not just pick up the phone for a random long distance call and personal trips were also extremely rare.

The adventurous newlyweds packed up and drove across country, moving to the high desert town of Mojave very near Edwards to embark on their life together. Dad and mom at first bravely settled with a couple of other NACA families into a tiny row of on base clap board apartments in the middle of the always windy, dry, dusty desert where drastic seasonal temperatures were the norm.

It was in Mojave that my rascally, older brother was born in 1949. Only a year later, my very Irish looking older sister, Patty, arrived. It was said she took after mom's dad with her blonde, red highlighted hair, freckles and impish grin. Soon after Patty's birth our little family moved to Lancaster into a larger home, the green house on Ave J-6 which provided room for the growing family. In 1951, the Air Force Flight Test Center was activated and I made my grand arrival, with all my spunkiness, as the final addition to their baby booming family.

When we were small, my mother worked part-time as a nurse in local doctor's offices and later at the local hospital. I remember the clinking of the glass and spoon as mom stirred the cold chocolate milk for me as I played 'Red Light, Green Light' with Sheriff John and she ironed her nurses uniform. Mom moistened her white nurses hat with heavy liquid starch, carefully folded it into a small compact square and placed it in the ice box in wax paper until she was ready to iron it perfectly flat. She then sprinkled the uniform with water using a Coca-Cola bottle with a shaker bottle top. I'd perch myself on the pale green, chenille bedspread proudly looking up at her as she readied herself for work, taking in her every move whilst sitting on the end of the wood framed bed, part of the six piece dark Mahogany bedroom set. The set, a wedding present to themselves has stayed in the family to this day.

My mother would smile when she looked at the matching mahogany and glass art deco picture frame which was included with the purchase. It held their wedding photograph and stood in the same spot on the mahogany dresser for as long as I can remember.

I'd watch with great interest the process of mom dressing in her sharp white uniform, pulling on her girdle. In the '50s girdles were not quite the tortuous, old-style, bone corsets but evolved to elasticized, slimming tubes which one slipped up over the feet and tugged up to the waist. Girdle coming from the meaning to 'gird ones loins' which explained the stuffed sausage feeling as it held in the stomach and buttocks firmly. Tight fitting contraptions extending from the waist to mid thigh where little dangling hook style buttons called garters, were used to attach and holdup nylon stockings. Girdles back then make Spanx of today look like comfortable body stockings in comparison.

After mom tugged on her white girdle she then carefully inched on white, seamed, silk stockings then gently hooked them on the garters front and back on each leg, slipped on and tied her white newly-polished nursing shoes, then dropped her full length white slip over her head, followed by the white, freshly starched nurse uniform. The Pièce de résistance the crisp nurse's hat which earlier in the day she had painstakingly prepared with heavy starch, ironed flat and crisp and now was intricately folded and buttoned into a perfectly pointed nurse hat. Finally, she carefully buttoned and painstakingly attached her special nurse pins. To me these were badges of honor. She looked so beautiful and valiant especially with the crisp nurse's hat folded to stand up high on her head as she bobby-pinned it just so behind her short tight curls. As I heard the sound of her white nurse nylons and shoes swish by, she would pat my head, kiss us each good bye and tell us all to "Behave" as she went out the door and off to work. She was a working mom long before Woman's Lib.

All that was left to do with her at work was watch Woody Woodpecker, Howdy Doody, Rin Tin Tin, Lassie or my favorite Zorro and, of course, the Lone Ranger and Tonto. Either the babysitter or dad looked after us. I loved it when dad was home to watch us as he always made things fun and we were allowed to run the neighborhood and play.

One very fond remembrance embedded in my heart was sitting with mom at the red and gray Formica-topped, shiny steel kitchenette table. My brother and sister played out back so I had her full and undivided attention. Mom was not an ostentatious lady so when she applied nail polish you knew it was a special night out on the town. As a nurse, the rules forbade nail polish so off it would come the next day; but this particular night she was preparing for a dance with dad.

Oh how my dad loved to dance and sing! There was always music in the house when dad was home... all types of music from Frank Sinatra to Tchaikovsky to the Glenn Miller Band, Lawrence Welk and Mitch Miller. Innate musicality came easy for dad, he sang in a Barber Shop Quartet in school and played the banjo. The polka was our favorite dance. Dad would pick all three of us up in his arms and dance around the room. We would all laugh and giggle. My favorite moments were when he held my hands while I stood on his feet and we'd dance, sliding and hopping around the living room to the polka music while the Lawrence Welk band played and bubbles filled the air in front of the orchestra on the black & white, box style TV screen.

My father's joy and zest for life was contagious and we never failed to erupt in gales of laughter and hugs at the end of the song. I always loved the last spin around the room as dad lifted me for the final chords of the music. It wasn't too long before I was an adept dancing partner traveling alongside him to the music.

This particular night my parents, the neighbors along with other friends and pilots from the base were going out to kick up their heels. I could feel the excitement and anticipation of the evening as mom sat in her terry cloth robe carefully applying her own deep red nail polish and as a special treat she was also doing my nails. I felt so rapturously grown up, just like mommy. While she painted my nails with the same red polish as hers, I examined the manicure set inside and out. Although it only appeared on special occasions, I knew every stitch of that magical box. Mom's well-taken-care-of manicure set, with an aroma all it's own, held all the tools needed for a complete manicure at the time. It had traveled from the Catskill Mountains of New York on board ships across the Atlantic with her to France and back and then across the country from the East coast to California and now sat on the '50s gray-topped Formica and steel kitchenette table with the bright red vinyl-covered, steel chairs where she shared its contents with me, her third little stair step. After her death, this manicure set would have a divine appointment, healing my grief of her loss by landing in the hands of a sweet, young college student and history buff, Stefanie

Martin, whose major interest was women of WWII. Eager to learn more about the lives of Army nurses, she enticed and pried stories out of me amidst my grief and sorrow. Relaying stories about my mother and father's courtship and marriage along with childhood family stories ultimately led to much healing from loss and the first step towards opening the door to writing this book.

Stefanie also took every email and story I sent to her and created an elaborate and beautifully-decorated photo album documenting my parents love and early marriage. I will be forever grateful to her for that amazingly thoughtful gift. In return, I sent her my mother's WWII nurse's cape as a Christmas present which she proudly added to her collection.

My parent's post-war frugality afforded the purchase of practical items of dinner ware and cookware as special wedding presents for themselves. A sturdy full set of everyday Blue Pacific, Winfield China with a delicate white bamboo design and a set of shiny, stainless steel, copper bottomed Revere Ware pots and pans were familiar old friends in our family kitchen for as long as I can remember. Mom spent many hours each day cooking full, well-rounded, healthy meals for her family. These were the days when baked potatoes were wrapped in foil and baked in the oven for over an hour, not set in a microwave for four minutes on a paper towel. Everything was made from scratch. There were no cake mixes in boxes or instant anything. Most of the time, these meals took all day to prepare. Some are still comfort foods for me today.

One of those meals was fondly referred to by dad as "Shit on a Shingle." Mom would scold him, "Marty, the children!" Then they would both laugh and giggle as they reminisced about how awful the Army version was lumped over old dry toast. Mom magically served up her yummy version for dinner with leftover Thanksgiving turkey, mushroom soup, onion and celery scooped hot over homemade waffles fresh off the electric waffle iron.

Every night the family would gather around the shiny metal dinette, sit in our assigned seats, bow our heads with hands reverently pressed together fingers pointed skyward, thumbs crossed, and together recite the Catholic 'Grace Before Meal', then share a meal and the day's events. We never lifted a fork or hand to start eating without giving thanks to God for all His heavenly blessings, a habit learned both by example and a hand slap or two. Every evening steamy meals of meat, potatoes and vegetables were served up on this now family heirloom blue Winfield China.

One of the selling points of the sturdy Winfield dinnerware was the claim that it was 'unbreakable.' Dad's compadres from work, our neighbors, were over for a fun family barbecue. Dad, who had a few bourbon and cokes, decided to expound on this selling point. I stood close by as he raised one of mom's precious blue cereal bowls high in the air, proclaiming, "See, it doesn't break when it's dropped!" All eyes were on him as he released his hold and it crashed to the patchwork black and gray, Formica kitchen floor. Roars of laughter pealed thru the kitchen. Dad's shocked look and mom's frown as she screeched, "MARTY!" gave way to many giggles, as dad said, "Well it's a good damn thing they promise replacement if it does break. We'll be taking them up on that."

Chapter 3

The Cloverleaf Rug

My first memories include the ever-constant giant wool throw rug that adorned our living room floor. As a bitty one, I had a close up view of the large green, cloverleaf pattern which served as my runway and landing spot before the wooden box, console, black and white, RCA TV each day. The cloverleaf family rug became an Irish lifeblood grounding piece as it traveled with us from home to home, and there were many, filling each new residence with continuity. When it was stretched out with furniture in place, along with the flying geese dad had made in furniture class that were carefully hung stretched in flight, then a breath of home was breathed into the sparsest of rentals. Here amongst the clover leaves I'd drink my Ovaltine chocolate milk along with Sheriff John, take part in Romper Room, enraptured by the Magic Mirror waiting for my name to be called, always disappointed when it was missed. My absolute favorite was Disney's Mickey Mouse Club and I knew each Mouseketeer by name. I felt a special affection for Jimmy and Annette as if they were close friends. Some nights, Jack Benny, his violin and Rochester filled the house with schtick and laughs as the family joined together in front of the tube on the cloverleaf rug. On Sunday nights, "The World of Disney" and Tinker Bell would fill our home with magic pixie dust while Davy Crockett filled our hearts and home with adventure, transporting us to far-off, wonderful places. Like many boys in the neighborhood, my brother donned a coon skin cap on a regular basis just like Davy Crocket.

Although I was the third stair step, the littlest and very shy, I could hold my own against my rowdy siblings. Because of my indomitable will to stand my ground with them, dad, dubbed me "Mighty Mite", after Mighty Mouse. A label I very much liked. If they dared me I usually took the dare. I made Herculean Superman jumps off furniture with my cape, a long towel or pillow case attached at the neck, flying in the breeze from around my shoulders, leaping off high buildings in a single bound to Metropolis below. My brother would dare me to jump off the roof like Superman and although I was ready and willing mom would inevitably intervene. I always thought it was so unfair Superman could only be a man or a mouse and was thrilled to learn there was a Super Woman, too. However, I was completely baffled and dismayed at the size of her tiny waist knowing I'd never measure up to her.

One of my favorite toys was my holster and guns where I could play cowboys and Indians just like Gene Autry and Roy Rogers for hours in front of the TV set on the cloverleaf rug. I was a top notch shot too, blowing the smoke from the barrel with each shot. Rarely did my siblings ever out shoot me nor did I allow them to claim they had. Yes I was Mighty Mite and I never let them forget it.

Even at a very early age we were all expected and taught to do chores around the house. Our beds were to be made every day along with dusting, keeping our rooms clean, picking up our toys, setting the table and helping with the dishes. Mom's Army nurse training never left her. For as long as I can remember she made her bed tight with hospital corners. Making a bed with mom was a learning event too. As small children, even at the age of five, we were taught how to make sharp hospital-style corners. Only perfect hospital corners were acceptable and with practice I became very adept at it. You couldn't bounce a quarter off my bed but I laboriously achieved a very nicely made, smooth and tight bed daily. Our beds were never left unmade and always needed to pass inspection. Mom's approval nod and small smile was all I needed to know I'd done a good job in my attempt at hospital corners. My efforts were most always rewarded with that smile. Today, I've relaxed quite a bit and no longer still make my bed with hospital corners; however every time I make the bed I see my mom's approving smile and fondly remember her teaching me perfectly-formed hospital corners.

Wonderful family vacations were taken each summer to the high Sierra's and Kern River. Some of my fondest childhood memories stem from the smell of the river, pine trees and campfires. Each summer, the call of the Sierras would beckon us. The family would pack up the car and drive across the dry desert, winding our way up into the Sierras where, nestled in the mountains, was an oasis, the Kern River. Melted winter snow waters rushing downstream over giant boulders and centuries old river worn rocks, pine trees and cotton woods simply everywhere. Here at the Kern River, pilots and government workers took refuge. Kernville, a quant tourist Mecca to the desert rats of the Antelope Valley and close by Bakersfield on the other side of the Sierras, afforded inexpensive vacations to those on a shoe-string budget. Summer vacations here were simply glorious. I remember these as simple times, running barefoot in our undies, sitting in river pools of cool water. No bathing suits required.

Dad was an avid fisherman and knew all the best fishing holes. He would rise before dawn and traverse the canyon and river in quest of dinner. We children quickly grew to appreciate the scrumptiousness of the fresh Rainbow Trout that dad victoriously caught, cleaned and mom fried up in corn batter.

Other grand and momentous family vacations which cultivated strong happy memories were our family trips to Disneyland in Anaheim. Here we would stay overnight in a motel, visit Disneyland late into the night one night and go back the next day to take in a bit more. Payment into the park would allow each family member a book of ride tickets; the orange E tickets were the very best and most exciting rides. For some reason, I had a great fondness and love of Dumbo. Dumbo was not an E ticket but the best ride to me. It along with Peter Pan enabled my imagination to soar along with the Mad Tea Party, Mr. Toad's Wild Ride and King Arthur's Carousel.

The Monsanto Home of the Future was amazing as a little girl as well. It was beyond imagination the things that were to come in the future... things today that seem silly or archaic now. Little did we know in our lifetime that the space program would take us far beyond what the Monsanto futuristic display conveyed in the '50s. Dad's favorite spot was the Golden Horseshoe Saloon where Slue Foot Sue and her dancers taught me the Can-Can dance and where mom and dad could sit, relax and have lunch. I'll never forget my first Jungle Cruise ride, mom getting splashed by the hippo water and the jungle cruise operator shooting a warning about a rogue crocodile and saving us. Sitting in the Tiki Tiki Tiki Room with my family taking in it's thousands of brightly colored singing birds was a joy as well.

My parents would ride each ride with us as a family or take turns if we were too small for the E ticket rides. I wasn't so interested in the Rocket ship ride, but Dennis loved it so I stayed back with mom while dad and Dennis rode it several times.

Disneyland had just opened in July of 1955 and our first visit to Disneyland as a family was in 1956. The Skyway buckets were a big draw for us. Every couple of years we would make a return trip for the most recent ride opening like the Matterhorn. On the second day of each trip we would always make our way to the pancake restaurant in Frontierland for scrumptious blueberry pancakes then spend the day playing on Tom Sawyers Island climbing the rocks, taking the rafts and canoes out in the lagoon or climbing in Robinson Caruso's tree house. Disneyland, 'The Happiest Place On Earth" brought the books, movies and TV shows we watched all year long to life in a very tangible, exciting way. The last day would end early in the afternoon and we would head home.

One time in particular, I had asked to ride Dumbo several times, but time was running short. Although shy and soft-spoken, when my heart was broken there was no holding back my disappointment and tears. This time, in a very public way I locked horns with mom. She took me by the hand firmly and informed me we had gone on enough rides, it was getting late and we needed to head home. Shocked and in utter disbelief that my requests had been denied while all my brother's had been fulfilled I insistently dug my heels in, loudly wailing, "But I haven't ridden Dumbo yet! I have to ride Dumbo! NO! We can't leave! You promised!" She kept tugging me along insistent we needed to go, hushing me, concerned about the journey home. Crocodile tears and giant sobs of protest escaped my tiny body, disproving that Disneyland was always 'the happiest place on earth' and making other couples very happy their children were quietly behaving.

Dad finally intervened as he would many times in our lives when our wills would clash. At his insistence, we walked back from Main Street as a family to Fantasyland in search of Dumbo. I have pictures dad snapped on his box Poloroid camera of us sitting in Dumbo, his big ears permanently frozen in air, flying wide as we rode 'one last ride', me with a tear streaked face, smiling, and mother determinedly frowning, only half smiling, giving dad the eye. Mom knew how to show both her unhappiness at dad undermining her insistence to leave the 'happiest place on earth' and her amusement at the change in my personality once I sat my tiny keester in Dumbo and started to fly.

Yes there we sat, me victoriously holding on ... flying with Dumbo.

Chapter 4

Brother – Dennis

As sweet as these moments were for me they lay at the other end of the spectrum from my brother, Dennis', antics which kept my parents hopping and caused many heart-stopping moments. I will never forget the sound of my mother shrieking, "Noooo!!" as she catapulted forward too late to stop my brother from swallowing straight pins he plucked from her sewing pin cushion. There was never any explanation given as to why he would do this. The memory of sitting in the doctor's office while x-rays were taken to see how many he had ingested still remains clear. We saved those x-rays and all had a good look at his iron man intestines while the whole family waited on 'pins and needles' to see if the straight pins, there were three, would be expelled in his excrement. I remember my father holding the x-ray up to the bright over head bathroom light as both my father and mother had the unholy task of searching for them in his poop. His bowel movement had become a family affair as all of us breathed a sigh of relief when every last pin was accounted for. All were grateful no vital organs were punctured and that episode was over so we could return to the normalcy of our World of Disney TV time in the living room to watch Tinkerbell magically flitter above the Disneyland Cinderella's castle sprinkling her pixie dust.

My brother was a ruffian who even at an early age loved to roll his short sleeves up James Dean style. He demonstrated for anyone who would watch how his black and white high top Converse tennis shoes could make him run faster and jump higher.

He wore his coon skin cap sometimes and other times he'd slap on the Brylcreem. "A little dab'll do ya" was the Brylcreem jingle, however, my brother practiced "if a dab was good a glob was better" as he combed his hair into a very cool, very slick 'duck tail' and wore his comb in his back jeans pocket James Dean style. He loved to play with candy cigarettes from the ice cream man and fireworks. One Fourth of July, we had been bathed, fed and were enjoying a visit next door to the Crossfield's backyard where all the children were given a lit fiery sparkler to celebrate the holiday. Dennis managed to catch my robe on fire with his sparkler. I escaped unscathed as it didn't burn for too long before watchful parents ripped the robe from me and snuffed out the flames. The Roger's, the neighbors behind us, unfortunately also discovered his love of fire the day he tried to set their redwood fence on fire with matches. It too was thankfully extinguished in time due to the dry tumble weeds sending up a Rin Tin Tin type smoke signal alert which summoned the parents from all nearby houses. They came running to douse the flames with buckets of water leaving only a black scorched fence in it's wake, which, thankfully for the neighbors, could only be seen from the desert side of the fence. One more time Dennis was led away by the scruff of the neck by dad after all flames were extinguished.

Then there was the time that the lure of the WWII Army trunk that held dad's war memorabilia was just way too enticing for Dennis and his cohort David Franklin, two curious comrades in mischief. One fateful day, they decided their mission was to climb up into the dark recesses of the garage rafters where, deep in a latched Army trunk, my dad had carefully stored away two Japanese Samurai swords he'd retrieved from his time served in the South Pacific and Japan. It may as well have been a buried treasure chest to these two budding engineers as they scrambled up on top of two saw horses. Then using blocks of wood and boxes eventually achieved heights needed to cling to the wooden rafters of the garage. Dennis hoisted himself up onto the rafter shelves, booty in sight, opened the trunk retrieving the swords from the safety of dad's hiding place.

Finally scrambling down to the cement floor of the garage with the score in hand, filled with elation, awe and wonderment, a closer examination was in order. While David looked on, encouraging his buddy to, "Open it!" Dennis decided he needed to pull the largest sword's outer casing open to reveal the gleaming, two sided, hara-kiri, war blade. He held it up close to his chest and pulled with all his might, it slipped up to his neck as the casing gave way revealing the ultra sharp, shiny blade which then sliced his throat as it slid out of its housing. At the sight of his partner's blood David let out a scream that would instantly alert any mother not just normal play was in the works.

Immediately, mom bolted out of the house in the direction of the high pitched scream to discover her son's bleeding throat. There she found him still standing in the garage with the blood covered sword in hand. She took one look, ascertained the situation and sent little David scurrying home. There was no 911 or paramedics back then and no ambulances were called in those days unless you were dying. As a nurse she kept her cool, examined the wounds depth and severity, then gathered up Dennis into the car, yet once again, she sped her son to the doctor office where she also worked on

Lancaster Blvd. only moments away. Driving with one hand, she held a clean cloth to Dennis' neck to help stop the bleeding as he lay next to her on the front bench seat of the car. Later, when asked why he would do such a thing, I remember him meekly stating a logical, "I wanted to see the blade." Miraculously no veins or ligaments were sliced. The doctor informed my mother and brother that he had miraculously just missed a major blood vessel. The cut was treated with sutures and a large white bandage wrapped around his neck. Dennis vowed NEVER to ever touch the swords again. He never did. He still has the 'war scar' to this day as proof of his curious mishap. 'The Japanese sword that slit Dennis' throat' as it became known in our household has gone by the wayside over the years in auction to a WWII sword collector.

Chapter 5

Sister – Patty

Mother and father were both proud, devout, Irish Catholics with strong Byrnes and Curran (mother's maiden name) family roots in Ireland. We were raised as such in church from the first day I can remember. Every Sunday without fail we were in church for Mass, a Catholic commitment, the reliable family glue which held us together as we moved from home to home.

Christmas and Easter were particularly special church times which always allowed for special shopping trips for new church clothes, specially chosen by each child. Some of my most special memories of all of us children are when we lined up for our picture in the backyard all bright and shiny clean, decked out in our new duds and Easter hats clinging happily to our Easter baskets. There were other times when bickering and fighting would break out on a Sunday morning preparing to leave for church. Many times, my mother in her dry Army wit would line us up like troops barking orders, "Line up! Now march! Hut, two, three, four. Come on let's go! Out the door! In the car!" I didn't like this marching scenario as I always seemed to be bringing up the rear, the last and the slowest to adhere to the Army marching rule which usually led to a smack on the bottom as I exited out the door or climbed in the car.

Ultimately though we arrived at church and all walked down the middle aisle, angelic stair steps in a line, together as a family to our pew seats. Every Sunday this was the drill. Then, at the appointed time, my father would leave us to take his place on the altar. He would sing the Mass hymns and responses in Latin while the priest said Mass. Latin was his second language, well learned in seminary.

My father was the most handsome man I'd ever seen and when he sang I could not take my eyes off him. He had gray hair by the age of 18, turning white gray by the time I was in elementary school, and his contrasting brilliant blue eyes created the most stunning effect, not aging him at all but on the contrary his love of laughter, jokes and storytelling revealed his true youthful, jovial side. He seemed to always be smiling. My heart would soar when he took to the pulpit to sing, hearing his beautiful tenor voice ring out across the church echoing praise to God. I knew everyone in the church was looking and listening to him but importantly and most especially I knew he was my daddy. I loved him beyond all measure. I'd often look at my mother in her elegant gloves and lace scarf in these times to see her smiling up at him as she sat in the pew next to me echoing my very feelings of love and pride. There were many times like this in my early years, wonderful, nurturing happy times. Although we had our troubles we had a loving home.

While still living in Lancaster my older sister, Patty, died due to complications while having her tonsils removed. The fifties were different times and many surgeries were done in the small town doctor's office under local anesthesia. My mother worked as a nurse for this particular doctor coincidentally his name, Dr. Burns, and trusted him implicitly. My sister's death on that table in the office where she worked was extremely devastating for her and for my family. By today's standards he would most likely have been jailed or sued for malpractice; however back then it wasn't an option. My mother chose to pray for him, forgave him and changed jobs.

Mom had only the year before lost another baby due to miscarriage and it was too much for her to bear. She let it be clearly known she wanted no more children so we were now the Byrnes family of four. The house was painfully quiet, an inexplicable emptiness seemed to hang over the house like a shroud. I was little, just four years old and my sister five when we lost her but I still remember a freckle-faced, high-spirited, mischievous girl full of spunk and energy who never seemed to stop talking or moving.

Memories of these days after her loss are dark. There was so much sadness and silence in the house, in the neighborhood. Although mom was a very strong woman, I don't think she ever truly recovered from the loss, as something changed in her. One thing I remember and cherish from those times was the camaraderie of all the neighbors pulling together to support my family in our time of need. The revolving gate had been nailed shut by now, closed off because the Crossfield family next door had moved to a new assignment and the new neighbors frowned on the children freely entering their yard. Still, the fence was the meeting ground to console, comfort and pass on baked goods and casseroles, a comforting staple in time of grief, or to hand me over the fence to loving friends who would care for me while my father, mother and brother attended my sister's funeral and burial, thus protecting me, saving me from the pain they felt I was too little to experience.

Chapter 6

The Bicycle

The Mojave desert has massive, dry lake beds and long before the Space Shuttle landed there the most colossal event happened for me in the early 1950's on one of these dry lake beds. Yes, gigantic indeed as my daddy taught me to ride my first bike training wheels free across the parched, flat desert. The Christmas before Santa had graduated me from my keyed, steel metal, roller skates to a bright red two wheel bike with a bell and training wheels. Miles were logged as I spent long hours riding up and down the driveway and street ringing that bell. My brother helped teach me to master clothes pinning playing cards to the spokes to make an engine sound while we rode. Then one Saturday daddy said, "Hey, Betty Bean, let's take a ride, just you, me and your bike. Oh and let's take off these training wheels. How about that?"

I was astonished and thrilled to have my daddy all to myself but the thought of riding my bike without training wheels terrified me. We drove in the car out to the desert, me on the front bench-seat next to daddy, windows down, the hot, dry summer breeze blowing inside. There were no car air conditioners in those days. My fear and trepidation abated as daddy loudly sang my favorite song of all time which still to this day evokes the deepest feelings of contented happiness and love. His beautiful tenor voice crooning,

♪ *"You are my sunshine, my only sunshine.*

You make me happy when clouds are gray.
You'll never know, Dear, how much I love you.
Please don't take my sunshine away." ♪

He'd tweak my cheek and give me a wink as he sang. Soon we arrived to our destination which was the middle of nowhere at previously named Muroc Dry Lake and then renamed Rogers Dry Lake, which was being used at the time by test pilots and ultimately ended up the landing ground for the future Space Shuttles.

Hopping out of the car I looked down at the dry barren ground. The earth under my feet was flat, parched and cracked and ran in all directions for what seemed like forever. As I picked up a piece of the desert floor exalting, "Look Daddy! They look like big dirt cookies!" he laughingly admonished me, "Well just don't eat it, Mighty Mite." Then he hauled my bike out of the trunk, took off the training wheels and said, "Hop on!" I trustingly obeyed even though I was so scared I could barely breathe. He assured me, "Now, Betty Bean, I'll be right here holding on to you and the bike. You just hold on tight and peddle as fast as you can. I'll guide you along." Through the fear and not wanting to disappoint him, I began to peddle with all my might as he ran behind me pushing the bike at first and then guiding it from behind with one hand. I picked up speed moving faster and faster. Out across the flat empty desert floor I rode and he ran right behind me shouting assuring words as we flew along at what felt at my tender age to be break neck speed, my hair flying in the hot desert breeze.

When I could finally breathe, I started to giddily exhale, "I'm doing it! I'm doing it!" Suddenly, there was no response, no return reply. Afraid to turn around, I looked forward yelling, "Daddy?!" From far behind me I heard him yell, "You're doing great. Keep peddling! You're on your own!" The bike wobbled as I realized I was on my own and then became steady again as I regained momentum and balance, peddling as hard as I could. Then he ran to meet me and showed me how to stop and turn. I rode for what seemed like hours, out and back and round and round, there on that dry river bed in the middle of nowhere as he supervised, laughed and encouraged me the entire time. Then we drove home, first stopping at the local Dairy Queen for a celebratory chocolate covered, Flying Saucer ice cream bar to reward me for great accomplishments of bike riding wonder.

We rode our bicycles with abandon with no thought of protection. You just better be careful and ride your best. If you fell you fell. No helmet, no knee pads as there was no such thing in the 1950's. We were a tough and daring generation with no frills such as protective wear. Compared to today's safety standards, it's a wonder we survived. One day, my little neighborhood friend who was skating down the street with me ate it. One minute she was up and moving along next to me and the next a wrangled mess in the gravely street. Her knees were torn up and bloody filled with gravel and asphalt stones. Mom came running when she heard our screams and cries and carried her into our bathroom to clean the wounds. She washed her knees over the sink, applying the magical red Mercurochrome elixir with the glass wand applicator, which almost every home had in their medicine cabinet. As I stood next to the sink and closely watched mom nurse the cuts and scrapes of my whimpering friend, I felt ill and light-headed. Remembering only the feel of the cold porcelain sink on my hands and the sight of blood, I passed out in the corner of the bathroom, thus learning very early in life the knack for my mother's nursing skills was definitely not in my genes.

One of my favorite songs, "How Much Is That Doggie In The Window?" by Patti Page was a popular and happy song that played on the radio regularly along with Doris Day's melancholy song "Que Sera Sera". This song's lyrics and melody, "Whatever Will Be, Will Be" touched a nonchalant place in my heart to dream about the future. I could often be found alone in the yard, around the house or riding my bike around the neighborhood day-dreaming and singing it.

Not long after finding the freedom of riding a big person bike, my brother hatched a plan with his cohort David Franklin. He led the gang, us three, and we rode into town and down the main drag, Lancaster Boulevard, so we could hit the drug store and the Woolworth's 5 and Dime. It was an amazing first time, exhilarating adventure for me and I rode like mad to keep up with the boys. Their bikes were bigger than mine which required much more peddling but puffing along and working hard, I held my own. We crossed all the intersections at the lights. Cars stopped to allow us to walk our bikes across the street which my big brother had taught me was the rule. It was late in the afternoon when we headed for home.

Exhausted and oblivious of what we had done as I was just tagging after Dennis on a fun adventure I was happy to arrive home. Upon arrival we set the kickstands and piled in the front door. There stopping us in our tracks, joined in a unified stance of disapproval, hands on hips like a fortress wall were both my parents. There they stood hovering above, glaring down over us.

Suddenly I was questioning the events of the day in my little mind. I'd never heard this tone in their voices before as they demanded, "Where have you been?" My brother bleated out that we had gone into town on a bike ride. They barked back, "And who told you that you could ride your bikes into town?" My brother responded with a sheepish, "No one."

The next thing I knew he was again being led out the back door through the backyard by the scruff of the neck and into the garage by my dad, who ominously clenched his folded belt in hand. In those days the belt was the answer to misbehavior and discipline. Today it would be the reason to call social services. I was shockingly terrified having never ever given my daddy a reason to spank me, let alone with a belt. I froze petrified as I was told, "You stand right there! Your next!" Hearing my brother's shrieks of pain after the sound of each belt thwack I could barely breathe, paralyzed with fear, it felt as though I was receiving each strike. Then dad marched my sobbing brother back into the house past me, telling him, "Now get to your room and stay there! There will be no dinner for you tonight!" Dad then turned his attention toward me, led me to the garage as tears rolled down my cheeks. Standing in the garage looking up at my idol, my daddy, I was in stark terror. This was a different daddy than I had known. I began crying hysterically as my eyes landed on the folded belt in his hand and watched him raise it into the air. Expecting the smack of the belt on my bottom or legs I blurted out through my tears, "I'm sorry daddy. I'm sorry daddy. Please don't hit me." He looked at me and lowered the belt and said, "Okay Betty Bean. I think you've learned your lesson. Don't ever go anywhere without asking your mom or me first." He grimaced saying, "Go on now. Run on into the house and go to your room."

I shot out of the garage and into the house like a bat out of hell and hid in my room. Both of us, in the end, did get our dinner as my mother thought it was too harsh to not only whip us but also withhold the dinner she had worked so hard on that day; however it was a very somber meal. I never forgot that experience. It would not be the last time my raffish, mischievous brother would receive the belt for some ill-fated scheme; however, for me, I learned tears definitely worked miracles.

Chapter 7

The Accident

One clear crisp autumn Saturday when mom was working at the local hospital, dad decided to take his little ones for a nice country drive up into mountains. The three of us piled into our family car, the 1954, turquoise-blue Buick with the three decorative holes in a row along the high reaching front fender on each side. We made a quick stop at Rocket Liquor Store, or more notably referred to by dad as "Vern's Watering Hole," said hello to a good friend of my dad's, Vern Door, the owner. We bought sodas and enough snacks to keep us going for the day. The front seat was a huge bench seat allowing ample space for all three of us with room to spare. I felt safe clutching my doll in between dad and Dennis who sat shot gun as I laid claim to the middle ground in front of the radio. There were no seat belts back then so we could hop about the car if something interesting came on the radio or even kneel or stand up on the seat to see out the window. Out across the desert we embarked on our journey, ascending the winding mountain road to higher elevation. Dad taught us tricks to pop our ears so we could hear better and avoid ear aches. We laughed and talked and my brother and I played 'you can't cross the imaginary line on the seat or you get to smack the other person's hand.' A game he invented, much smacking took place and for some reason his line always kept moving closer to me.

Higher and higher under the brilliant blue Southern California sky we climbed into the Tehachapi Mountains. I loved these trips, even at the tender age of six; road trips appealed to my adventurous spirit. To me, we were explorers covering unknown territory seeking new horizons. The quality of air smelled different here than in the high desert where we lived and there were far more trees. For some reason I loved red houses and always searched for and inevitably made dad laugh when I successfully spotted one on each trip exclaiming, "I want to live in a red house one day!" The radio played and we all sang along through the desert but soon we lost transmission in the mountains. Of course that was no problem as dad would just switch off the static and sing. To me he was far more entertaining than the radio anyway as he gestured in an Italian way and sang,

♪ *" When the moon hits your eye like a big*

pizzzza pie ... that's ... Amore!" ♪

We were all singing along now and laughing. One minute we were having a fabulous joyous time and the next minute dad was yelling, "Hold on!! Hold on!!" He stomped on the brakes over and over but nothing happened. The brakes had failed and the car was careening down hill out of control. He turned the wheel back and forth then suddenly and abruptly we slammed into a telephone pole, dead stopped on the edge of the road. God had stopped our speeding decent as we came out of a downhill turn and a near-fatal accident using the same telephone pole that dad had stapled his picture to the year before while running for the seat of Lancaster assembly man, a position he didn't win. However the telephone pole came in very handy at stopping tons of run-away steel and metal. He joked later that the city made him pay to replace the telephone pole and asked if his picture would be on the new one as owner.

Cars had no safety standards back then, no cushioning anywhere. The dash board was metal, shaped in a very cool futuristic point which in accidents became a horrific weapon of destruction. The giant steering wheel was also a battering ram in these instances. My brother and I had flown up off the front seat onto the dash board. He escaped unscathed with only a chipped front tooth. I however flew up into the dashboard and stopped it with my forehead. I had a three inch gash in my little forehead and was bleeding like a sieve. The bottle of orange pop I had been drinking and held between my legs at time of impact had sprayed everywhere. I was more upset about the sticky orange pop than the blood. I heard dad saying I was in shock.

Dad had taken a very bad hit on the battering ram steering wheel which punctured his bottom lip and took out several teeth. He gathered himself, checked us both, made sure we understood completely not to move from where we were or open the car doors as he drug himself out of the car. Forever my hero, he ran down the hill for help to a lone house that looked to be occupied. As God would have it, the occupants were home and had a phone which was not always the case in those days. While still in the car waiting for dad to return, my dear brother pointed out the window to a cavernous valley floor far below where we had nearly met our doom saying, "Look, Bets, we almost ended up down there."

The image of that canyon floor became indelibly seared in my memory as I peered over the window edge to the deep valley below. I jumped back from the window and sat safely on the seat where I could hold on. Still today I get very nervous on mountain roads cliff side. I have often wondered if my fear of heights did not develop from this turn of events.

This time, an ambulance was in order and soon it arrived sirens blaring. I remember asking my brother if that sound was for us as I heard the siren getting closer and him turning to look up and out the back window nodding his head at me. Dad was loaded on to a gurney and into the ambulance first. Gripping tightly to my doll, they laid me on a gurney and attempted to strap me down; however my biggest concern was where they were taking my daddy. They wanted me to lay still but I needed to know where he was and kept fidgeting trying to sit up and turning to look for him. Then I heard him say, "I'm right here, Betty Bean. It's okay, Mighty Mite. I'm right here."

Finally realizing he was next to me in the ambulance he reached out from his gurney and held my hand all the way to the hospital, telling me jokes about the hole in his bottom lip to keep me from falling asleep saying, "Now I'll be able to squirt milk out of this extra hole." I tried to smile... knowing his new hole in his lip was much more serious than that, I responded, "Oh Daddy you're so silly." After close examination of my brother and ascertaining he only had the chipped tooth, he was given the privilege of sitting up front with the ambulance driver and assigned the important job of pushing the siren button. I am sure that siren never ran more than on that day.

My mother who was on staff at the hospital working that day was not happy to see that the accident patients being wheeled in were, in fact, her own family. After losing her daughter the year before, she became distraught. My mother was not a demonstrative person but on this day she hugged and kissed my brother and me, caressed my head and hand comforting me, going between rooms affectionately checking on us all repeatedly. I rarely saw my mother cry but that day I remember seeing her dressed in her sharp white nurses uniform as another nurse held her in her arms allowing her to cry heart wrenching sobs. She seemed to have a new found gratitude and love for her husband and her little brood this day or maybe that was just the first time I saw her love and concern for us so clearly.

It took many stitches to close my forehead wound. In those days they were less concerned about cosmetic closure and to me the stitches looked like a black, hairy, caterpillar worm on my forehead. It wasn't long before I was recouped, returning to school where the children had fun teasing me for many months about the 'third eyebrow.' To this day I still wear my hair over the scar. My dad had a dental bridge made to replace five bottom teeth he lost that day. Many times he entertained us (well maybe not mom so much) over the years by flicking it out with his tongue to show it off and for many years continued to tease and joke about the hole in his bottom lip.

Chapter 8

The Announcement

Then came the night which changed our lives forever. Even at my young age I knew it was an important night. We could all feel it in the air. My dad's boss, Walt Williams and his wife, Shirley, were coming over to make an announcement. They had never visited our home before or, at least, I never remembered them visiting.

Mom covered the picnic table with a red and white checkered table cloth. Dad lit the straw basket covered wine bottle candle with the many colors of candle drippings down the side and set it on the picnic table in the backyard. They fixed drinks and set out hors d'oeuvres. My brother and I were bathed early and dressed in our snuggly pajamas for bed. Mom and Dad told us to watch TV and that we were not to go outside while the grownups talked. I remember sitting all sparkly clean, obediently on the long green divan which was positioned in front of the living room, tangerine-orange wall dad had creatively painted and on which he had hung the three black wooden geese.

We knew something important and exciting was happening and were not about to be left out so we mischievously crept over to the smaller green divan which leaned up against the large window to the backyard. Quietly, we snickered and giggled while we peered out through the venetian blinds spying to see what was going on.

Dad and mom were there in the backyard candle light along with Mr. Williams and his wife. He was a robust and animated man with a full head of thick hair similar to my dads and going gray. His loud boisterous voice carried so we could hear him saying what seemed to be important things. They all seemed very happy, laughing and patting each other on the back. Smiling big, the meeting adjourned and they dispersed, taking leave walking by us through the living room. As they left, Mr. Williams patted us on the head and Mrs. Williams gave us hugs and pinched our cheeks, talking about how cute we were and how we'd grown so much before leaving out the front door.

As soon as the door closed behind them, my parents looked at one another and then back to us telling us it was official; we were moving to Virginia so daddy could work at Langley Air Force Base and Mr. and Mrs. Williams and their family would be moving there too.

Before long the house was packed and we said goodbye to Lancaster. It was a very long drive across country to Hampton, Virginia, the town dad grew up in.

Dad was taking his family of four ... home to Hampton Virginia

Betty Byrnes

PART 2

Virginia

Land of Forests and Beaches

Langley

There's music in the sighing of a reed;
There's music in the gushing of a rill;
There's music in all things, if men had ears:
Their earth is but an echo of the spheres.

~ Lord Byron

Betty Byrnes

Chapter 1

Hampton, Virginia

Leaving behind Edwards Air Force Base and the dusty desert city of Lancaster, our little family packed up to undertake a long excursion across country to the Atlantic coastline in Virginia. Suitcases and a few toys all packed into our bulky, sedan, we traveled as the majority of the U.S. population traveled in the '50s and '60s. Not many years later, Dinah Shore sang "See the U.S.A. in your Chevrolet"... and that is exactly how we saw the U.S.A., by car.

All our belongings traveled across the country by moving van to storage, so we took our time on our road trip, taking in the sights like the Grand Canyon and many other tourist spots, stopping regularly to pile out of the car and stretch our legs at various rest stops like Stuckeys and Howard Johnson's along the way, each day mapped out and ending with a motel stay. One of our favorite things to do on the drive was to read the signs along Route 66 which advertised endless motels with flashing neon signs offering swimming pool fun. Our motel pick was always a fun, lively family decision. No reservations were necessary to make in advance back then. To our delight, if the weather was warm enough, after a long days drive, we would take a night swim while mom and dad enjoyed a cocktail near the pool on the aluminum chaise lounge chairs.

Although rest stops and tourist stops were fun, very rarely did we eat in a restaurant as mom always opted for home cooking even on the road. So there were many picnic table stops and 'tail gate' lunches. The sturdy, silver, family Coleman cooler, filled with motel ice, was put to good use on these long family trips across country. However, even the cooler couldn't keep all food fresh for long, as I found myself sick one early morning after breakfast when mom had inadvertently fed me bad leftover canned pineapple. Needless to say, to this day, I'm sketchy about left over pineapple.

Dad had his agenda and plotted out the miles to cover each day and not wanting to stop was considering the time lost for a 'wee wee' stop in the bushes. I remember him glancing at the mileage and looking back over the front seat as I sat turning green in the back seat, complaining, "I don't feel good."

Mom was saying, "It's ok she must have a bit of car sickness. Just keep going."

I was saying, "Daddy, I think I'm going to throw up."

Mom took another closer look at me and told dad to pull over, jumped out, opened the back door where I immediately blew chunks of morning breakfast. Mom felt terrible as any mother would. There is a big line between being thrifty and accidentally poisoning your children. We laughed about that incident many years later.

During this drive across country my mother took advantage of seeking out her WAC Army buddies she had ardently kept in touch with, stopping at their ranches and homes for warm reunion visits. These lovely, strong women remained faithful friends of mom's whom she communicated with by letter. Mom kept the dying art of letter writing alive her entire life with an endless stream of cards and letters to family, friends and everyone she ever held dear.

This move to Virginia would be the first of several moves as the child of a NASA family in the early years. I can sympathize with children of military families who move with each new assignment of duty. I remember sadly watching from the backseat as costumed 'trick or treaters' ran gleefully down small town streets we passed through. Looking at their smiles, bags and buckets filled with candy in friendly neighborhoods I yearned to be planted somewhere. Watching with my nose pressed up against the glass of the back seat car window, happy memories flooded in. Ironically, I had been a gypsy the year before and just knew I had the best costume on the block. The sounds of laughter and running exuberantly from door to door on the Lancaster streets filled my mind. Absolutely amazed and thrilled when mom had come up with the idea and allowed me to wear her Army nurses cape and jewelry over a bright red dress topped off with her bright red lipstick. The cape was adult size, one size fits all, long before that became a label, but I was determined it fit me perfectly. It was a dashing dark blue, heavy wool cape with a dark, maroon red, wool lining which hooked and buttoned at the collared neck. Mom had worn it on board ship while on duty in WWII. I felt special and oh so mysterious. Gallantly impressive to the neighborhood children's "ohhs and ahhhs" was my Zorro cape flip into the air. I remember my mother smiling as she buttoned it at the collar and said, "There you go, fits perfectly." The heavy weight of the wool barely lifting in the breeze behind me while running from house to house. I was marvelously impressed with my costume, much more so than the bag of candy I collected that year.

All normal life stopped for each new move. Making friends was always difficult for me. I was painfully shy in new situations spending long hours playing alone, not that I was lonely. If I did make friends, loosing the new friends was even more painful with each new move. My relatively solitary childhood fueled my imagination, creativity and artistic abilities as they became my close companions and a huge outlet for me ultimately sparking an interest in the arts, creativity, crafts, sewing, knitting and clothes design in later teen years.

In Hampton, Virginia, it was no longer just the four of us as I met the large Hickman family for the first time... my father's sister Aunt Mary, Uncle Cecil and their brood of five children. Shyly and gingerly, I navigated my way with new rambunctious playmates, slowly getting to know my five cousins at family dinners in their whitewashed, two-story, 1900, turn of the century, clapboard house. This was my dad's childhood home, the house he grew up in and from which he left for seminary college. He'd only been back once with mom to visit his family since their marriage when Dennis was an infant and before Patty or I were born. His father and mother, my grand parents, were now gone. They had both died while we lived in Lancaster and a visit to their graveside was taken so father could pay his respects.

Watching out the backseat car window we sat very still and quiet while dad stood graveside, his hands folded and head down praying. His lips moved as he talked to his parents or God or maybe both. The old house had been left to Aunt Mary after they passed. I'd seen pictures of mom and dad with baby Dennis on Grandma's lap. She had a small weak smile and seemed ill but happy to meet her grandson. My Grandfather was a stern, unhappy looking man and I always wondered how my jovial, outgoing father had ever been related to such a person. This old house seemed so secure, comforting and permanent to me compared to our family who was in nebulous transition. I often wondered if it was Aunt Mary who had made it that way, as my Victorian Grandparents didn't seem to bring much joy or comfort to the place from the stern look of their pictures. It was old and drafty, the wood floors echoed when you walked yet it felt comfortable and homey for them. I was fascinated when cousin, Peggy, let me in on her eavesdropping secret, directing me to stand just under the ceiling air vent at the bottom of the stairs in the dining room, parlor area while cousin, Bobby, clambered up wooden stairs to say a few words to his older sister, Hanna, in their parent's bedroom, thus revealing you could hear everything that was said upstairs clearly without ever leaving that spot.

Exploring the yard and standing under the magnificently huge Pecan tree that had been there forever was magical. Everything was wide open here in this quaint old neighborhood. There were no sidewalks or curbs like in Lancaster. The streets which were roughly paved were bordered on each side by big gullies where the rain washed down the street in the winter. There were no fences here except at the back property line behind the garage where the back alley lay. The green grass carpeted yards were massive. Aunt Mary dressed in her full apron while standing over the sink washing potatoes and cutting green beans for dinner at the sunbathed kitchen window, regaled us with stories about dad's task of mowing the expansive half acre spread of grass with a push mower when he was a boy. She smiled at dad and he shook his head in a "that's just not right" joking manner when she shared that his nephew, Bobby, the fourth child, mowed it with a gasoline powered mower. They laughed together over old memories of growing up in this venerable old house. Their kindred laughter translated to my heart. I sensed dad's roots here in this place and attached my heart as well.

A tiny, white, slatted, matching clapboard garage sat in the back yard, separate from the house to the left under the Pecan tree at the end of two long narrow ribbons of concrete leading from the street which I soon discovered while out walking with dad was the drive way. Dad explained this type driveway had worked just fine for my grandparent's Model T.

Peering out between ivy-veiled chain link behind the garage, the alley looked both ominously scary and mysterious, especially when my cousins, with a giggle, successfully teased and frightened me, telling me not to ever go there because it was 'very dangerous'. I shuddered and kept my distance, not wanting to know why or what they were giggling about.

Aunt Mary was thrilled to have her brother home and the whole family thought my dad was the best thing since sliced bread and fawned all over him. Dad was a wonderful story teller and they all clamored around him on each visit to ask for the latest story about whatever was on his mind. He could pull a story out of his hat in a New York minute.

Sadly I never met any of my grandparents and little was ever said about them growing up. It was only in later years, while homeschooling two of my own children for a genealogy class, we were to learn from mom the history of my grandparents.

Dad's parents first met and married in Philadelphia, where they both lived in the early 1900's. They moved to Hampton, Virginia to settle and raise their family. Both strict devout Irish Catholics, grandfather labored in the shipyards and his father was an engineer on the railroads that ran the East coast. My dad's mother, my grandmother, Elizabeth Loretta Durgin Byrnes, suffered severely with arthritis and was wheelchair-bound for at least a decade before her death. I was named after her and my mother's older sister, Aunt Elizabeth Curran. My dad's father, Martin Aloysius Byrnes Sr., my grandfather, was a harsh 'take no nonsense' type man with a strong Irish will. Grandfather Byrnes had not taken well to dad's desire to fly, to enlist in the Army and serve his country. It was only later in life that I learned he did not want dad to marry. His father's life-long dream for his son was that he become a priest. For me the perception of my grandparent's Victorian outlook was a complete juxtaposition to dad's jovial, outgoing personality. It seemed he broke free when he went into the service and never looked back. Yes, this was Virginia, the land of my ancestors... hard working Irish Catholics, who labored building ships in Norfolk shipyards and engineered the locomotive trains running the East coast rail lines. It is no wonder my dad's love of flying was first birthed in this place, the bustling hub of all types of industrial transportation.

My mother's mom, Katherine Henrietta Bradley Curran, my grandmother, was a lovely warm woman of sturdy Irish stock, her roots and family from County Tyrone, Ireland. She was the adventurous sort and didn't hesitate to take the trip to the US when it was offered. Her brother, my great Uncle Robert Bradley originally left Ireland to escape the great Potato Famine. He sailed across the Atlantic and settled in Philadelphia where his hard work allowed him ownership of a hotel. He scrimped and saved passage money for grandmother's older sister to come and join him. When the time came, he sent a ticket for passage; however, she was too frightened to travel alone and leave her home in Ireland. So adventuresome Grandmother Curran, impetuously jumped at the chance. She readily packed a few precious belongings into a suitcase and took her older sister's place, traveling by sea in 'potato boat steerage' to Philadelphia where she joined her older brother, Robert and tended the hotel. It was in Philadelphia that my Grandmother first met Grandfather Curran, John William Curran, both were devout Irish Catholics.

Mom grew up in a similar Victorian wood clapboard house as dad's but twice as large... a two story home with a large open front veranda porch in the Catskills of Upstate N.Y. where her parents as newlyweds moved and settled down to rear five children. Mom became adept working in the yard from a young age doing manual chores around the property to help provide food for the family, as she and her four siblings helped tend the large property. The Lavender tree behind the house was her mother's favorite and brought her much joy and beauty in an otherwise drab existence. As a teen mom helped maintain it and pruned it for her every year. Mom's face would soften as the sweet memory crossed her mind sharing how her mother relished to see its beautiful full lavender-blue blooms each spring.

Mom was a very athletic child, an avid crackerjack basketball player. She could out play any of the neighborhood boys. She grew up with three sisters, Francis, Elizabeth and Gertie and a brother, Bill. She was the youngest of the brood and the only one allowed to own a pet, a beautiful long haired collie, named Shep which became the family dog; however her prime responsibility. When she left for nursing school, her sisters faithfully cared for Shep.

In the winter her sisters, brother, cousins and neighbor friends would ice skate on the local frozen lakes. It was dangerous recreation, at times. There were sad stories of treacherous mishaps where cousins fell through the ice and died.

As a child, I would peer curiously at wonderful pictures of mom happily sitting with Grandma holding Dennis as a baby in her lap on the porch of her childhood, Tannersville home.

Mom's dad, my grandfather, was a conscientious carpenter taking any jobs he could to provide for his large family. He was very Irish looking with auburn red hair. My mother would shake her head and roll her eyes the few times she spoke of her father. He had a reputation for fun living. In pictures he always looked somewhat like a leprechaun to me with his narrow face and straw, brimmed hat. He was a mover and a shaker very proud of his Model T Ford. Mom shared stories of being deathly afraid of traveling in her father's flimsy car. Seems the entire family had piled in for a first time ride through the countryside in order for grandpa to show off his brand new open air Model T, the Curran family's very first ever car. Puttering down the road she abruptly and unexpectedly fell out hitting the ground hard as a result of the door latches not working properly. Grandfather Curran loved to party, a hard working Irish Catholic man who lived hard and worked hard. Seems my mother was attracted to my father for the same qualities that presided in my grandfather. Although Dad never met Grandpa Curran he always reminded me more of Mom's dad than his own stern father.

Chapter 2

Henry Street

We found a new temporary home in a somewhat more modern 1930's white two story, clap board slatted house on Henry Street in Hampton not far from Aunt Mary's. Henry Street was lined with giant elm trees which created a soothing canopy in summer and turned brilliant colors in the fall. Similar to Aunt Mary's, this house also had a sunny kitchen at the back; however a sloping, shingled roof running the full length along the front of the house was adorned with two, protruding, storm windows, like two large eyes looking out over the front door and mud room. There were large storage spaces in the side walls upstairs which made for wonderful hiding places, private forts in our own bedrooms. I set up my portable orange record player in my fort and spent many hours listening to 45s of children's music. My favorites were Roy Rogers and Dale Evans' "Happy Trails to You" and the Mickey Mouse Adventures.

My room had a slanted ceiling making one wall shorter than the other which gave me the feeling of sleeping in a giant doll house. To enter the house you had to climb several thick cement steps front or back as the house lay on a raised foundation allowing for snow in the winter. Just outside the kitchen window, much to both mine and mom's delight, lovely yellow daffodils pushed happily up out of the ground every fall. The daffodil garden provided a lovely place to sit and day dream, 'Que Sera Sera'. Like all the older homes a separate wooden, one car garage sat off to the left in the backyard attached to the two long thin concrete ribbons leading in from the street; albeit these ribbons were a bit thicker and wider than Aunt Mary's. As time went by and cars grew sturdier the ribbons of concrete were widened some; then, eventually became a full cement drive. Here, too, at this house were massive yards; however a row of tall thick bushes lined the property separating us from the right side neighbor's house. On the left lay an exact duplicate white wood slatted house as ours where the Hamparian family lived.

The Hamparians were also a NASA family and Mr. Hamparian worked on base with dad. They owned a fabulous swing set much like the one we had left behind in Lancaster. Many long hours were spent creating amazing childhood feats on those swing sets, performing gymnastic prowess in shows for obliging grown ups, who clapped at all the appropriate times if they happen to be paying attention. Summertime evenings in Virginia turned into magical events as the fire flies came out to entertain us. The squeals of happy, rambunctious children echoed through the yards as we ran haphazardly, capturing the glowing creatures in jars with holes poked in their metal lids. Holding the jars up close for inspection, their glowing entertainment kept us busy for hours, ultimately, though, we always set them free of our make shift lanterns hoping they would live to enjoy the hunt for another night.

We were not settled yet and as much as I begged for a cat or a dog my mother would not allow pets so I was happy to find at this house there were lovely neighborhood cats who came to visit. My dad referred to these as "those silly ole' alley cats" then secretly fed and provided them a kitty box in the garage where they could escape the harsh, cold Virginia winter. They became my regular companions. The Hamparians, a fun loving, friendly, loudly raucous family of Armenian heritage quickly hit it off with my parents. At the back of their property, behind their garage was a chicken coup where the hens provided fresh eggs which they freely shared. Horrifyingly for me there was also a large tree stump that served as a butcher block. It held an axe at the ready for when it was time to hack off their heads and pluck them for family dinner. This only happened once while we lived there when a hen would no longer produce. Thankfully we were spared witnessing this event. I steered very wide and clear from that area of the yard.

Many family parties were shared in our backyards. Although we didn't have too much in common, I loved playing with their older daughter, a quiet, sweet girl several years older than me; however their knockabout son, Randy, two years older than me, was a pushy, brash kid who did not impress me, by any means. He loved to tease and taunt me endlessly. He was not the least bit afraid of anything, even intimidating my brother with some of his antics. One of my brother's chores was to rake the fall leaves in the yard into a large pile for burning in the incinerator which sat at the far back corner of the yard. One day, to my horror, while standing with my dad on the backyard stoop, supervising my brother's leaf raking abilities we watched as Randy shared that he wanted to show us a trick he called, 'The Cat Bomb.' He picked up one of the visiting cats, my favorite black cat, and much to my horror, carefully placed him under a large mound of multicolored fall leaves. Then, with all his might he vaulted himself into the air landing hard on the protruding cat's tail sending the poor creature yowling, screaming, flying high into the air with an explosion of yellow, orange and red leaves everywhere. He rolled on the ground with laughter at this as I stood stunned and stricken, at first, then screaming in protest, flew away running after the cat to see if he was hurt. My dad laughed, shaking his head side-to-side in disbelief in a 'no' motion saying out loud, "That Crazy Hamparian kid!" For many years to come he talked about that, "That Crazy Hamparian kid!" To this day, my brother still mentions that sick but funny Hamparian kid's 'Cat Bomb.' Still to this day... it brings only a wry smile, as I still don't find it funny.

One quiet, peaceful, fall, afternoon weekend, dad jumped up, shot out of his chair and ran out the back door with an alarmed look on his face. Dennis and I followed suit, trailing after him... running outside to investigate an unusually loud revving noise in the backyard. There we found Mr. Hamparian, a big man with a giant grin, peering out the side window, waving madly, whilst hunched over and crammed into a brand new tiny Volkswagen Bug. At the time, it was a unique, little, round German car newly released in the states post WWII and Mr. Hamparian had just bought one for his family. Like a big, gleeful kid in a soap box derby car he was showing off how easily it maneuvered by driving in circles round and round on the grass in the backyard. Around the swing set and down the drive way and back again, round and round he went punching the peddles and revving the engine. Dad, with a very surprised look on his face, was laughing like crazy while he shook his head from side to side saying, "What the hell is that? Good Lord, it's just nutty Hamparian! Come out here and get a load of this, Katie! He bought a Volkswagen Bug!" We all stood on the back stoop at a safe distance watching the dizzying driving stunts while Mrs. Hamparian stood on her back stoop waving her apron, nervously smiling, pleading, "Stop it! Stop it now!"

Not long after this stunt my parents were inspired by the new economy, compact cars on the market to trade in the big, bulky, family sedan with ginormous, silver bumpers we had driven across country in for a much smaller, newer, white, Ford Falcon. My parents were always practical and never bought brand new cars, always, instead opting for used cars, just a few years old. I learned from my mother you must always pull the choke button out and pump the gas peddle just so in order to start this Falcon car. Sometimes it would start quickly; other times not and sometimes it would flood if the gas was pumped too much, which could be especially irritating on freezing cold winter mornings. There were not many colors to choose from in those days. Unlike today your typical paint choices were black, beige, brown or white. Mom always chose white. All subsequent cars after the Falcon were also white for many years. Her reasoning which held up was that white was easier to keep clean and stayed cooler especially on hot summer days, as built in car air conditioning had not been invented yet.

If you had the luxury of an air conditioner, which we did not, it was a loud portable contraption fueled by smelly gasoline which slid over the window while rolled up and barely kept the air cool. Our type of air conditioning was rolling down the windows while driving and putting our face to the breeze or opening the triangle shaped, side window vents and pointing them inward as we drove.

Down the street on the corner was a tiny store where we could buy candy, Tootsie Pops, and Bazooka bubble gum for a penny and small toys with our allowance. I spent endless hours chewing Bazooka bubble gum and loved the 'Bazooka Joe and his Gang' comics inside, learning to blow large bubbles skillfully so as to not allow them to pop and get stuck in my hair... a skill I adapted to quite well. Nickel jaw breakers were my brother's favorite, the bigger the better. Most impressively he could decimate a giant jaw breaker, which barely fit in his mouth, in a few days and would display them in his grubby palm showing me the changing colors as he went along, saving them bedside for each next day.

The Mattel Barbie had just made its arrival into almost every little girl's world. I had been given my first Barbie doll with the black and white striped bathing suit for my eighth, November birthday; however it was up to me to buy Barbie doll clothes with my allowance. I was told that I must earn them. Diligently, I went about my chores setting the table, making my bed, cleaning my room, dusting, helping in the kitchen and around the house to earn my quarter allowance each week. Endless hours were spent combing through the little book which came with the Barbie doll dreaming and wishing for sets of Barbie clothes for her. Then, finally, after saving for several weeks, making several trips to the corner store to suss out which Barbie outfit would be the perfect purchase, after counting and recounting to make sure I had exactly the right amount of money, $1.43 including tax, with my mother's permission I walked down to the store on the corner and selected the Barbie outfit I could afford. Then, I proudly bought it and some candy, with change leftover. Already longing and planning for the next Barbie outfit before ever leaving the store. Barbie became my passion and soon Barbie's wardrobe had grown, as I collected many outfits and accessories with my allowance, filling up a shoe box to over flowing.

Crushingly the children in the Lancaster neighborhood burst the Santa bubble the summer before taunting me for believing in Santa Claus.

Tearfully I ran home to verify this abhorrent lie as fact with mother. This Christmas following my eighth birthday, I decided it was time for me to take my allowance and ride the bus into town alone to buy my family Christmas presents. If there was no Santa Claus then I needed to step up and make sure everyone received a gift from me, after all, it had been all up to my parents all those years to put those presents under the tree. I asked mom for permission and she gave me explicit instructions on what bus to take, what time I needed to be home and which stores I could visit (something that would never be safely done today). She buttoned up my navy cardigan sweater, tied my oxfords securely, made sure my Timex watch with the black leather band was buckled properly on my wrist and synchronized with the red framed, electric, kitchen wall clock then, waved goodbye as she watched from the road while I walked down the street under the canopy of the giant elms to the bus stop on the corner near the little store. Boarding the bus alone, I had little trepidation, felt fearless and grown up as I climbed the bus steps and dropped in my bus token. Sitting in the front close to the driver, I rode the bus, speaking only to a few ladies in black hats and short day gloves just to say, "Good morning ma'am." They each smiled and nodded back.

Downtown the bus ambled along, jerking to a stop to let passengers on and off then, finally stopping at my first destination the busy Hampton, AM&PM grocery store. After much searching for just the right color I bought a bright red, thick potholder for a nickel for my mom, deciding she would need this as she cooked so much. Then at the Five and Dime I garnered the perfect gift for my brother, a Paddle Ball, which looked like a ping pong paddle with a rubber ball attached to it by a long rubber band. Recounting the money in my change purse I tried as I might but could not think of anything to buy my dad with the amount of money I had left. Then, a light bulb went on that dad spent much time in the garage building things. He was handy with wood and whenever a new bed frame was needed for growing children or other furniture was needed he would build it. So I headed off on the bus once more, destination the hardware store; even though it wasn't on mom's list of stores, I just knew she would understand. Here at the hardware store, I found his perfect gifts.

Arriving home, I explained to mom I had to go to an extra store to get dad his special present and, thankfully, she smiled and understood. Quietly, I went to my room and carefully wrapped each item with simple white tissue paper and tape, tied a bright paper ribbon around them and placed them carefully under the Christmas tree. I couldn't wait for Christmas morning to see their faces. With the mystery of Santa Claus revealed, we now first celebrated Christmas by attending midnight Mass the night before, then woke early in the morning to gather in front of the Christmas tree to open presents. The awe and magic of walking out with bleary eyes to gaze on what Santa had magically delivered and inspect how many cookies he had eaten during the night was now gone; however in it's place was the joy of giving and receiving. My parents retained the serendipitous magic of Christmas for me as my eyes landed on a sweet blue eyed, Pollyanna doll in a blue dress and straw hat standing at the foot of the Christmas tree, her arms held out straight toward me as if waiting for a hug. Three feet tall, she was almost as big as me. We first each eagerly opened our presents from mom and dad one by one, receiving two or three presents each. My parents exchanged their gifts and shared hugs.

Then, it was finally time for everyone to open my presents to them. I was thrilled to see my brother happy with his paddle ball as he proceeded to bounce it all about the living room over everyone's head. Then it was mom's turn. Sitting at my parent's feet, I anxiously watched as she carefully removed the tape, as would be her way of opening presents her entire life. She never wasted a piece of paper, ribbon or cord, carefully removing the tape bit-by-bit, preserving the paper no matter the size of the present for future use... a frugal trait she learned living through the Depression. Finally she revealed the pot holder. She smiled at me brightly calling me, as always, by my full southern name. Her words wrapped around my heart like a warm hug as she expressed, "Oh! Betty Ann, this is just what I needed." Then it was dad's turn. His eyes sparkled, he smiled a big rakish grin even before he opened his gifts. Giving a wink to my mom, he held up three little presents to show her, each wrapped separately. Looking at me he chuckled, "Now what do we have here? Is this for me? I wonder what you've gotten me, Betty Bean?" Then he opened the first little package revealing a container of tiny nails. He roared a jovial, rolling, belly laugh and said, "Well I'll be darned if this isn't exactly what I've been looking for. I can use these with my hammer!" I was ecstatic pressing him, "Open the others, Daddy!" He opened each package revealing more nails and tacks all very tiny in their two inch tall, round, clear plastic tubes with the red caps. He roared with laughter with each newly, revealed handyman's present, finally taking me up in his arms and giving me a big hug. While I sat on his lap, he held the little tubes in his hand looking at them with great admiration. He kept those tubes of nails and tacks for years in his top dresser drawer and whenever I'd be in the garage with him I would ask, "Dad, are you going to use the nails I gave you this week?" He'd smile and say, "Not this week, Betty Bean. I am saving them for something very special."

This same Christmas, my parents gave me a rectangular, white vinyl covered Barbie storage box with a handle and gold tone clasp at one end. This was the very first Barbie carry case Mattel made. There were colorful pictures of Barbie stamped on the front in outfits I knew I just had to have for her. I can still smell the plastic and hear the sound of the clasp when I think of this box. Vinyl at the time was a new popular rubber type plastic material which came out after WWII in the late 40's and was everywhere by the mid '50s. I filled this case with all my hard earned Barbie outfits. There was a place to lay one Barbie inside and a little slide out compartment drawer for Barbie's accessories, also little pink Barbie hangers with a hook at the top inside on which to hang them. Barbies were a large part of my life for many, many years to come. Soon my collection would out grow this Barbie box. I kept this collection well into my twenties until mom passed it on to another little girl from church to enjoy. I would learn to sew and knit while making Barbie clothes and made many clothes for her. Then, I graduated to making my own clothes and sweaters in high school, designing and sewing clothes for myself and friends in the Hippie LOVE child era of the '60s.

Never sure what my daddy's work at Langley Research Center, Langley Air Force Base, Virginia was exactly, it was clear it was important and people liked him. One time which was very rare, in fact the only time I can remember, he took Dennis and I to the building where he worked to show us his office. He guided us on a tour of a low one story building deep in the Virginia woods that seemed once inside to go on forever. It was a modern decor with contemporary chairs in black leather with dark wood paneling everywhere. It was all very secretive and soldiers guarded the entrance.

Looking at my father's desk with eight year old eyes it was enormous. There was a nice lady in a pretty dress with a full crinoline skirt, a wide belt cinched tight at the waist, straight seamed nylons and pointy high heels with tightly coiffed blonde hair and painted nails who greeted us at dad's office door. She introduced herself, bending at the waist saying hello to each of us and asked if she could get us anything. Dad laughed and said, "No, I'm just giving the kids a tour of their old man's office." She was, as it turned out, his secretary and her desk sat outside his office just down the hall.

The inside hallway revealed many very large, full length windows. It was fall and the windows allowed for a full view of fall foliage. Thickets of trees arrayed in beautiful, orange, red, gold and purple foliage caught my attention and would not let go. Living the first few years of my life in the desert I'd never seen anything like it. Like a painting, I was mesmerized by the beauty.

In the not to distant future I was to learn this assignment at Langley Memorial Aeronautical Laboratory for NACA would become the nation's future space program, National Air and Space Administration (NASA), which would be instrumental in eventually landing the first astronauts on the moon; for now, though, I was just in great awe of dad's giant desk and the beautiful leaves seen through giant glass walls of windows.

Chapter 3

Buckroe Beach

While in Virginia, although we moved again, we went to the same Catholic church and school, St. Rose of Lima. After Henry Street in Hampton, we moved to the town of Buckroe Beach. This beach house was more affordable for our family at only $85 a month rent for a three bedroom home just a short distance to the beach. Here I was introduced to the joys of the beautiful, windswept, grassy hilled sand dunes and salty sea waters of the Chesapeake Bay. Swimming in the ocean waters of the Chesapeake Bay and walking the sand dunes on family picnics was a favorite weekend event. Many exhilarating, joyful hours of swimming were spent in these waters. It was here I learned to dodge jelly fish and dive under shore bound waves with abandon. My confidence grew as I became skilled at searching out the perfect wave to ride to shore. I remember many wonderful beach picnics and the laughter from mom and dad while sitting on the beach blanket as they enjoyed family, friends and fresh sea air. The vision of dad's admiring smile and his cheerful voice still echo in my mind, "Betty Bean, you sure swim like a fish!"

In Buckroe, the vacant lot which ran along one side of our home was not a desert but an over grown forest acreage filled with incredible giant birch trees, a thick blanket of intertwining ivy growing everywhere. To the right side, between the neighbor's house and ours, was a flat, well mowed, grassy half acre stretch of land where hours of football games and gymnastic feats were accomplished. Perfecting the cart wheels, somersaults and back bends even pulling mom outside to cartwheel with me many times.

My brother, in good neighborly fashion, was assigned the chore of mowing the giant stretch of grass just as dad had done when he was a boy, only Dennis used the neighbor's power mower. Behind the house, not too far from the backyard, a swamp flowed and an inlet stretched inland from the swampy waters, allowing fingers of water to creep up the property line toward the house. My imagination piqued while exploring these forest and swamp wonderlands with a few neighborhood children but mostly it was just me and my brother setting out on exciting adventures like Mark Twain on the Mississippi. We hiked for hours exploring, hunting for frogs, tadpoles and salamanders, collecting chigger bites and berries. I would turn many a hike into a Nancy Drew mystery in the recesses of those ivy forests.

Increasing our exploration horizons, my parents surprised both Dennis and myself with beautiful, new, shiny Schwinn cruiser bicycles. Dennis received a red boy's bike and mine was a light green girls bike. Now, within easy reach, only a bicycle ride away, was the beautiful Chesapeake Bay. We often rode our bikes into the town of Buckroe Beach to explore the beaches and stores. It was here that I found my favorite hat that summer, a white sailor hat with red stemmed cherries embroidered on the front which read, 'Life is just a bowl of Cherries.' Dad and I chuckled many times about my sailor hat which I bought with my allowance, wearing it for several summers in a row with pedal pushers or plaid Bermuda shorts, sleeveless white cotton shirts and Keds, low white canvas tennis shoes.

Here on the Buckroe boardwalk sat the most amazing old regal Victorian hotel, the Buckroe Beach Hotel. As dad rose at NASA, it became his joy to occasionally treat the family to brunch or dinner out in upscale restaurants. This old restaurant had well upholstered tapestry furniture in the lobby, finely appointed china and pristine white table clothes. One Sunday, after church, while still dressed in our church clothes with hats and gloves, dad took the family here for brunch. This was a place he knew of as a boy and he reminisced with us while stiff alert butlers with water pitchers and silver coffee pots fussed over us. Dad explained the restaurant had been a dance hall for the elite once and many dances took place there. As I listened to the china and silver clinking around me my imagination ran wild. I carefully ate my scrambled eggs while my mind drifted. Gazing up at the high elegant chandeliers filling the giant dining room and then glancing out the wall of huge picturesque pane glass windows overlooking the bay and boardwalk, I day dreamed of a dance hall filled with beautiful elegant couples in long gowns and gloves, holding elaborate fans, high hats and bow ties, delicately bowing and curtseying to one another, swaying about the room to orchestra music. Much to my dismay, we ate there only once for Sunday brunch, as my mother's frugal tastes ran to simpler places with less budget impact or just plain simple, practical home cooked food.

The adventuresome and the budding engineer that he was, Dennis, became very adept at making wooden rafts to float in the swampy inlets which lay behind the house. Much like Tom Sawyer, he would maneuver them between the reeds and cat tails with a long pole. He learned quickly to spot furry Muskrats and Water Moccasin snakes moving through the swampy water, a skill he taught me while riding his rafts. We rode bikes for long, endless hours along the back beach dirt, gravel roads while exploring, climbing trees and building tree houses. My brother climbed a big tree in the backyard and hung a rope and we swung like Tarzan over the largest inlet, competing to see who could give the loudest Tarzan yell. He always won.

Dennis taught me the art of throwing and kicking a football, which I took to quickly. One Sunday after church, still dressed in my gray, wool, tube skirt with the little slit in the back I grabbed the football to kick it high up and over the house which was our practice and landed flat on my back. I dissolved into hilarious giggles as I realized my skirt had inhibited my ferocious tomboy kick, knocking my feet out from under me, landing me flat in the grass on my back. Even my brother laughed at my surprised thud and shocked uproarious laughter.

My absolute favorite thing to do was to hike into the forest, find the most overgrown ivy vines connected to two or three tall Birch trees, climb to the top of the ivy and then slide down... voila instant slide. Who needs a playground when you have a forest? A child's imaginative wonderland.

Returning from the store one day, my mother took me outside with a pack of Zinnia seeds, where she helped me clear a small area near the front stoop for a garden. That was the summer my joy of gardening took root, as I meticulously planted the seeds patting down the earth over each firmly, daily filled the watering can keeping the barren ground moist. Within a short time, miraculously, I watched the seeds sprout and grow, the buds giving way to large daisy type blossoms in vibrant orange, pink and yellow. The long-lasting flowers always grabbed your attention and brought a smile to everyone's face as they climbed the steps to enter the house. I loved it when dad would smile approvingly and compliment me on my gardening skills, "Betty Ann, these are some pretty flowers you have growing here." Flowers in the garden still bring joy and peace to my life today.

On one of Dad's many long trips away from home, after learning about and seeing the beautiful horses in the neighboring Virginia countryside, I decided I just must have my own horse. I spent hours preparing hand written words and drawing what I felt were exquisite horse pictures then, rode along in the car with mother to the airport as she drove to pick up dad, asking her over and over, "Do you think dad will let me have a horse?" She was non-committal saying, "Well, you will just have to ask him."

I'm not sure why I would think that my parents needed to buy me a horse when we were not settled enough for a cat or a dog; however, my greeting for dad after the initial hug was a persistent, relentless sales pitch lasting almost the entire drive home, all keyed to a set of handmade flash cards, which I one-by-one held up to display for him, pleading for him to buy me a riding horse, stating various reasons why this would benefit me, the family and the horse. He was extremely patient to read each card in between words of conversation with my mom, enduring the entire presentation after his long business trip. Several times I saw him eye mom with a questioning look. I felt I was getting through and was beaming with self approval at my presentation skills.

Dad, glancing back over the back seat while mom drove took in my entire presentation, words, pictures and all and then, I wrapped it up, very pleased with myself belting out, "Well, can I have a horse?" He then gave a final, loving but very firm answer, "No. You may not have a horse."

Instead I received horse statues on birthdays and returning business trips. However, after ceaseless begging it was here in Virginia my parents allowed my deep desire and dream of riding horses to come true. I learned English riding at the stable in the forest back roads of Virginia. My favorite horse was a calm, gentle Michael Landon, Pinto horse just like Little Joe's on Bonanza. I had a love affair with horses for many years after our second summer in Virginia. My room became filled with horse statues and astronaut pictures.

This particular summer every waking moment was spent learning everything required to take my riding lesson. Sitting in the stables with the smell of hay and horses surrounding me watching others learn to ride while I memorized every part of the horses' body, their gear and equipment. This memorization was my test, which I passed with flying colors before I could ever climb on top of a horse for my first riding lesson. There, in the horse corrals on Virginia back roads, I spent every waking moment possible riding and jumping. Feeding the horses carrot treats, cleaning the stalls, walking and brushing them and cleaning their hooves was simply a sublime treat. The smell of a horse and barn still evokes many fond memories of times at the stable with the wind in my face as I trotted, galloped and cantered around the arenas, riding and jumping.

The large Officer's Club on base afforded fun and memorable Virginia family outings. Mom faithfully paid the family Officer Club dues of $5.00 a month. The Officer's Club swimming pool brought out the show off in my brother, who would do daring dives from the high board. I'd bravely climb the ladder to the high dive; then, my fear of heights would kick in and I'd crawl back down the ladder relegating myself to blissfully doing jack knives, cannon balls and front flips off the low board. We'd swim like fish for hours while the parents sat under the fringed umbrellas at round, metal, picnic tables slathered in Sea & Ski suntan lotion, enjoying their beer. Then, we'd dig into the metal, Coleman coolers for Wonder Bread and bologna sandwiches wrapped in wax paper, to end the day in a group blanket picnic on the lawn.

On occasional Sundays after church we would visit the Officers Club for brunches where impressive smart uniformed officers and their families ate there with us. Smiling waitresses in starched white uniforms and crisp ruffled aprons would offer us refills on our eggs, bacon, toast, juice and donuts. Mom was always amazed at how many refills we could eat. At home, we received one serving per meal, maybe seconds occasionally. At the Officers Club it was as much as we could eat on Sundays and we took full advantage of the special tasty treats.

Chapter 4

STG Brings Big Changes

It was 1958 and Project Mercury had begun. The Space Race had technically begun a year and three days after the Soviet Union's 'Sputnik I' flew its orbital space flight. According to my dad's notes, everyone in the NASA team at Langley took it as a challenge when they heard the words from a Russian cosmonaut challenging the U.S. with, "Where are you, Space Yank?"

My father was assigned the task of NASA Space Site Selection as assigned by the Presidential Advanced Committee Panel in Washington, D.C.. In Virginia, Dad made many mysterious business trips. It seemed he was gone a great deal of the time. He traveled to Washington D.C. on a regular basis and then off to many other places including Canada, White Sands; New Mexico, the Bahamas, Florida, Texas and even Alaska.

An especially enjoyable treat were the family business trips to Cape Canaveral, later to be named the Kennedy Space Center. One memorable trip was during the MA-1 rocket launch. It's here in Florida we would meet up with the Williams clan and have fun swimming and playing at the hotel pool and on the beach, while keeping up on the latest news of the rocket launches. We would all pile into one car and drive together for long trips out across the Florida beach landscape. We learned it was not a good thing to cram two families into one car and then drive the longest most desolate bridge in America. Things got a bit sketchy as claustrophobia and crankiness set in for some. It was during these family business trips that the dad's would spend the time for rocket blast offs at Cape Canaveral working at mission control and we would stay back with the mothers at the hotel listening to the TV, transistor or portable Motorola radios for news on the rocket launch. In between news reports, our favorite radio DJ's would spin the latest records. Our life completely revolved around space flights. These blast offs were always especially tense times; everything would stop as we would listen intently with the transistor radios up close to our ears or watch glued to the TV sets in the hotel rooms or at home. Intense concentration followed by absolute relief and celebration after safe take off was assured or slumped shoulders and hope for another day when missions were scrapped because of poor weather. I would always ask about the monkeys and worry for them to come home. It wasn't until I was older I learned some did not fare well during the first rocket launches. Then, they believed it was for the good of the country. The Space race took precedence over animal's lives. It was a different time. There were no animal rights groups then.

Dad was my north star, my guiding light. Although there was plenty to keep us busy, I missed him terribly when he was gone on trips; however, reunions were sweet and the presents he brought were always special, unique and wonderful. Even better, though, were the kisses and hugs, just having the family together again. I still have some of those presents, tangible fond memories, tucked away safely to this day.

I was to find out not much later why he traveled, as he was a member of the Space Task Group (STG) for NASA Site Selection assigned to study relocation programs. It was from the research and studies he performed that Houston, Texas was decided on by the heads of NASA and ultimately President John F. Kennedy as the home for NASA headquarters.

On one of his away trips, things became extremely frightening as Hurricane Gracie headed our way from the Atlantic Ocean. We were left alone, just the three of us to ride it out. We all felt extremely grateful our rented beach home sat on a high raised cement foundation. It was a long rectangular, one-story house with redwood clapboard siding which sat long ways on the narrow property with no garage. A long closed in porch ran almost the entire length of the house on the left side. The roadway to the house was a high raised dirt and gravel road with deep ditches on each side. Our driveway was a stubby gravel road connected to the front of the house which covered a large cement, drainage ditch pipe. The house sat high enough to be even with the raised road. With the onslaught of hurricane warnings on TV news and radio, my mother called us in. I can still hear the urgency in her voice, "Dennis!! Betty Ann!! Get in the house now!! Bring your bikes in too!" The way she called us I knew I wasn't in trouble because she would use my full given name for reprimand, "Elizabeth Ann." However, I knew by the tone of her voice she meant business and we moved quickly to get to the house. The weather was ominously overcast with dark clouds moving in. The rain had begun, the winds were blowing hard as we followed her direction bringing our bikes up the stairs inside to the enclosed porch. She bravely and resolutely took out the masking tape determined without hesitation to do whatever was necessary to help us stay safe. I learned strength from my mother. She taught me whether a woman or a man you just do what needs to be done. As best we could, we helped mom tape the house windows cross ways from corner to corner, then up and down, then rolled down and locked the levered patio windows and screens. We then went inside and closed the drapes and curtains to ride out the hurricane. The winds became stronger and stronger whistling like a freight train, the skies unleashed torrential rain beating down on the roof. She made pop corn and brought out cookies and milk to try to lighten the mood; however the howl of the wind and pounding of the rain on the house was deafening and we had no appetite for snacks. Not even the Sunbeam bread that tore a straight line down the middle and made fantastic cinnamon sugar toast could distract us from the raging storm. She kept us, all three, huddled in the living room on the green divan away from the windows watching black and white TV shows, switching occasionally to news reports to track the hurricane.

Then, finally, the electricity flickered and went out completely. Mom retrieved and lit candles for light. We played cards attempting to stay busy playing Fish and Concentration. The swamp water rose higher and higher. The deep ditches filled with swampy sea water and rain. The little finger of water that ran alongside the property soon became the entire swamp several feet deep in our backyard. Just when I thought the wind would never stop howling it suddenly became completely still. There was no sound outside. I asked mom, "Is it over? Is it gone now?" Mother told us we were in the eye of the hurricane where there is no sound, no movement, no wind. Here you do not ever hear birds chirp as they usually don't survive. It was an eerie feeling I didn't like. You could hear a pin drop. It was daytime yet there was an eerie darkness outside. We ran to peek out the windows at the back of the house to see the swamp had swelled up and invaded our backyard. I shivered thinking of all the Muskrats, Water Moccasin snakes and other creepy crawling animals that may be lurking in the water. My mother and brother laughed when I asked if there was some way we could find a boat thinking if the water rose any higher we would not be able to drive our Ford Falcon anywhere... that is if the wind hadn't carried it away. There was no way of knowing without going outside to look at the front of the house and I was too frightened to do that. Then, just as we finally relaxed with the calm of the storm the wind began again just as mighty and strong as before as the hurricane continued to pass over us. By now, it was night fall and the sound of the wind seemed much more fierce than during gray daylight. We waited and waited in candle light until finally it was over. We had survived our first hurricane. There would be more to come but for now the waters receded, the sun came out the next day and normal life went on. We had lots to tell Dad when he returned home.

During our time in Virginia I learned for the first time about prejudice. We always attended parochial school wherever we lived, my parents driving and picking us up daily. One day, while driving home from school, dad and I had a deep discussion. Being so shy, it was not easy to break through my timid barrier of self protection, so I was crushed and bewildered when a little boy in my class I liked was not allowed to play with me. My father, who loved all people had written his thesis in Latin while in seminary on the subject of integration in the 1930's long before the Civil Rights movement began. He was lending a sympathetic ear to my young frustration. The Negro boy I wanted to play with had a great big smile and contagious loving spirit. He was fun and friendly. We hit it off right away. I was excited, looking forward to recess to play with him outside on the playground. As the bell rang I instantly yelled, "Come on. Let's go!" However, my hopes were dashed standing in stunned disappointment as the nuns instead, giving me a scolding look, led him off by the shoulder in the opposite direction. Confused, I stood frozen in my tracks watching as all the Negro children were walked to a separate play area and were made to play on the black, hot, asphalt parking lot where basket ball hoops were installed, while all the white children played on the playground under the shade trees with the tether ball, monkey bars, swings, merry go round and sand box.

It didn't seem right to me and I asked dad, "Why?" He asked me, "What do you think about it? Where would you like him to play?" The answer seemed obvious, me telling him, "Well with me and the other children on the play ground." I had never experienced segregation before. There were no Negroes as African Americans were called at the time in Lancaster, California. He attempted to explain it to me in a limited and careful way but I was not having it. Further he didn't sound like he liked what he was telling me. I was adamant with my objection firmly telling him, "Daddy, I don't like it." He shook his head up and down nodding in agreement and I knew he felt the same; however I saw fear and concern in his eyes. He rarely ever became so serious with me. Now, I know attempting to protect me from ignorance and bigotry he said, "Honey, you need to obey your teacher and not speak of this anymore except with me or your mom." I remember feeling so disappointed and angry that my hero could not fix or change such a wrong situation. It was only as an adult after he passed away that I found his Latin thesis about integration written decades before the civil rights movement, which confirmed he understood the struggles of civil rights and affirmed how we were raised to love everyone no matter the color of their skin as we are all created equal in God's eyes and should treat each other as such.

While I was busy exploring forests, windswept sand dune beaches, watching Dick Clark's American Band Stand on TV, getting to know each dancer by name while dancing along, playing with Barbies or horseback riding in the back country of Virginia, NASA's space flights became manned. It was April 1959. I remember my father victoriously sharing with us that there will be no more monkeys or chimpanzees going up in rockets. It will be a manned space flight from here out. There would be seven test pilots chosen and they would be called 'astronauts'. Suddenly Project Mercury had begun. The first true 'Rock Stars' in my life were the real modern day pioneers and space explorers; the seven original astronauts: Walter "Wally" Schirra, Donald "Deke" Slayton, John Glenn, M. Scott Carpenter, Alan Shepard, Virgil "Gus" Grissom, and Gordon Cooper. A new NASA vocabulary took hold across the country: astronaut, Mercury, NASA, Cape Canaveral, Mission Control, launch pad and more were all now household words.

There was talk with the pick of the first original seven astronauts about Chuck Yeager who remained back at Edwards in Mojave. Test pilots were a tough and rowdy partying bunch. As the story goes, Yeager was a long time death defying, test pilot who had earned a reputation for being over-the-edge as a Fighter Ace in WWII. Even as test pilots go, he had an even tougher reputation. He was the first test pilot to break the sound barrier. Dad confided to mom in my presence that many were not happy about his actions when he learned he was not to be one of the chosen seven. Dad, shaking his head in disbelief while speaking of Yeager, emphatically said, "A damned foolish stunt to pull." Yeager who was one of 'the' top test pilots at Mojave at the time vied for a place with the chosen seven. Rumor has it, in his arrogant disappointment, anger and darn right defiance, under the dark of night he took a jet out of the hangar and flew at supersonic speed up and outside the earth's atmosphere and then back down to earth, proving, if only to himself and possibly theoretically in history he had become the very first U.S. man in space; albeit also ruining all chances of ever being chosen as an astronaut in the future. Sadly, they stated, at the time, he was too old to make the cut yet later much older men flew into space. However, Chuck Yeager ultimately led a long and illustrious career in the Air Force.

Dad had traveled to many places sussing out the details of many locations to see if the area, city or land met the criteria given to the STG for the location of the new NASA Research Center (the exact criteria is listed in dad's memoirs at the back of the book). They were looking for a place that would fulfill the needs of moving a massive amount of people and equipment with access to the ocean or a water way... a new home with room to grow in which to house the research needed and complete the space mission. He met government officials, governors and mayors and city chamber of commerce members across the country and in U.S. provinces. They took him on land site inspections as he interviewed the political powers in place at the time recording all the pertinent details. He then objectively prepared proposals forwarding all the information to his boss Mr. James Webb in Washington D.C., the second Administrator of NASA from February 14, 1961 to October 7, 1967, as he ultimately held the weight of the decision on his shoulders. Those results and that decision were then forwarded to President Kennedy who gave the final approval.

Mother's heart was longing for the high desert of California which had become her true home and held memories of her happiest times. She deeply vied for and hoped the decision would be made in favor of California and was greatly disappointed she could not return 'home.'

We gathered as a family, sitting pensively on the divan in the den of our rented Buckroe Beach house. Dad happily made the announcement as mom sat silently... our new destination, Houston, Texas.

I, on the other hand, held no fondness for the dusty, dry desert and was thrilled and delighted to hear that Texas was a land of horses, ranches, cows, big horned Brahma bulls and rodeos. I'd never been to a rodeo and I was ready. Surely, Texas was a horse lovers paradise. Dad promised me and mom shook her head in agreement, "Yes, we will find a place for you to ride horses in Texas! This time you'll be learning how to ride Western style!" Before long we packed up and embarked on our expedition back across the U.S., half way across the country to a new, completely different, exciting world.

The land where NASA was to be built ...
Houston, Texas.

Moon Child: Growing Up NASA

Betty Byrnes

Part 3

Houston

Land of Rodeos and Astronauts

NASA

"Music in the soul can be heard by the universe"

~ Lao Tsu

Betty Byrnes

Chapter 1

Houston, Texas

Collectively and with great gusto, the Byrnes family answered the call for Dad's new assignment in Houston, Texas where he would have many titles, but ultimately became the first manager of NASA, named assistant to his boss Walter C. Williams who was just appointed the first Director of Flight Research at NASA. Filled with high hopes for a bright future, our family once again packed into the family car and rolled on down the road on the all American road trip across the U.S.

A great tedium breaker and my favorite thing to do whilst traveling across country by car on these long road trips, other than playing with silly putty, reading MAD magazine, Superman, Archie and Little Lulu comic books and playing backseat games with my brother, was to sing as a family in the car, with dad always leading us in chorus. Another fun past time was reading the creative Burma Shave signs dotting the sides of long stretching highways, little signs on sticks, each one telling a new part of the story, always silly and ultimately selling Burma Shave. Dad would always warn me, "Hey, Betty Bean, here come the Burma Shave signs!" I'd perk up in my seat and set my paper dolls aside for a few moments to read each one before it flew out of sight. Everyone in the car would read the little signs out loud together if they weren't snoozing and laugh with each one. Another fond recollection are the Howard Johnson and Stuckey's rest stops and gift stores. Always a place to gas up the car, use the restrooms, stretch our legs, mingle with other road-weary travelers and buy silly trip mementos and postcards. Those orange roofs were always a welcome sight to our restless, cooped up, traveling family.

Again, mom arranged to visit one of her many WAC friends, who were spread out across the U.S. This time, we were welcomed with warm, Southern, Louisiana hospitality as her friend greeted us under giant trees covered in hanging moss. Her visits with these strong, astute, independent women were always lively, picking right up where they had left off years before. Having stayed abreast of each other's current life events by letter, long hours were spent chatting while sipping coffee happy to be in each other's presence before moving on to our final destination. I listened to their shared sisterhood while sitting at the steel dinette just like ours that everyone by then seemed to own in the '50s and early '60s. They talked for hours while I played solitaire, ate chocolate chip cookies and drank cold milk. The warmth of their love, friendship and hugs were memorable and nurturing for me. The fact that they valued me, never talked down to me but always included me in their conversation at some level would stay with me for a lifetime. I also learned about a fun loving, carefree side of mom which I did not normally see as I watched her interactions with her WAC friends.

This particular visit with mom's old WAC friend, whose children were both boys my and my brother's ages happily lasted a few nights as our parents enjoyed visiting and we pursued Huck Finn type activities. Sleeping bags were pulled out and a huge free for all sleepover occurred, pillow fights and all. The next day led to an adventurous, swamp excursion where teaming schools of tadpoles were just asking for closer inspection. Wiggling tadpoles along with an occasional frog were captured and released. Their home lay just off the fertile Mississippi River, where inviting, muddy inlets of dark green, murky water and reeds created magical, low lying, wildlife exploration areas for inquisitive, adventurous kids such as ourselves. The boys were eager to show us these fun-filled wetlands and we were just as excited to visit them. We had never met before but instantly bonded over the magnetic call of the frogs in the distance. Our excitement rose as we took off on foot hiking down the road where the sound of ribbitting frogs was echoing. My brother and I chattered on about his Huck Finn raft adventures in Virginia. Soon we were splashing ankle deep in Mississippi mud water. Squeals and uproarious laughter echoed through the inlet as we captured frogs and tadpoles in temporary holding jars to examine them up close. The tomboy in me simply reveled in this feat. Upon returning home after a long wet, adventurous, amphibian filled day, we feasted on a hot scrumptious New Orleans family dinner. Then, after warm baths followed by a good night's sleep, we said a cheerful thank you and goodbye and rolled on toward our final destination.

In nothing flat, we arrived in the cowboy land of guts and glory – the land most befitting the cowboys of the "Final Frontier." Dad, having served on the Presidential Advanced Committee Panel in Washington, D.C., was greeted with much regalia in Houston. There is a saying, "A cowboy is a patriot" and this is exactly how it felt in Houston. NASA was filled with space patriots who had answered the call to travel to space and back. There were the astronauts, the country's space cowboys, and all those working diligently behind the scenes. All incredibly intelligent, brilliantly talented and gifted men accomplishing super-human feats without the aid of computers or satellites.

In today's computer oriented society, the average person may not always understand the degree of intelligence and super-human attention to precise detail that was necessary for pioneering space flight to take place. Handwritten calculations and notes stemming from the work of the human brain and human reasoning were the bedrock entered into the only main frame computers used, giant monsters filling a large room at Cape Canaveral in Mission Control. There were no desk top computers or easily accessible computer programs. It was all manual configuration from the human brain. Here we find the true meaning of the term, "You don't have to be a rocket scientist to do this." For in fact they most certainly did have the brightest, most brilliant minds of rocket scientists from all over the world working on the rockets that launched the space capsules.

President John F. Kennedy had been elected in 1960 and sworn into office in January 1961. Our family being Irish Catholic was beyond ecstatic with our new President and First Lady. They were elegant, handsome, beautiful, fashionably chic and they were 'Irish Catholic'. They were 'our' special, relatable presidential family. The same year in October 1961 the ground breaking had taken place at the Houston NASA Space Center and the construction of buildings was moving forward quickly. Mission control or the command center remained at Cape Canaveral, Florida, later named the Kennedy Space Center. Dad took active participation, assigned facilitation of the building of the NASA offices and space center in Houston, inspecting blue prints and visiting the building site to observe the work. He wore his personalized NASA hard hat that all personnel on site were required to wear, including the astronauts when visiting the NASA building site. Dad's NASA hard hat always held a prime spot in Dad's NASA collection.

Dad fell into the latter category of brilliant men who worked behind the scenes at NASA and he was privileged to pave the way for the NASA contingency with our early arrival in Houston. He had written up the final proposal presented for ultimate approval by President Kennedy for the placement of the NASA Research Center in Houston and as a result had also been chosen to be the forward liaison for NASA. Being the first to arrive he was honored at many state and city dinners and parties where he established the foot hold for NASA public relations. He was the featured speaker at several events across the state and attended press conferences, TV interviews and parties as the guest of honor including a special dinner reception in Austin with then Governor, Price Daniel.

Dad was the NASA representative the day the agreement with Rice University, Texas and NASA Research Center was signed by Governor, Price Daniel. The mayor of Houston gifted him with a Stetson Cowboy hat in a large round Stetson box which I confiscated over the years and now has a place of honor in my collectibles today. At one large event he was given the key to the city and showered with gifts: door stops, a beautiful leather bound book of poems (which was my very favorite), engraved BIC lighters, ink wells, pens, hand-blown glass cocktail stir sticks, dinners and much more. Dad received an honorary invitation to ride as a VIP guest in the Pasadena Livestock and Rodeo Parade and another from the Mayor of Houston to attend and ride as the VIP guest with his family in the 1960 Houston Livestock Show and Rodeo Parade.

Riding as the featured NASA celebrity family in the Houston Rodeo Parade required the proper attire. Our first shopping trip in Texas for western wear allotted me a very interesting new, surprising perspective of mom as I watched her feisty gumption in action. Mom's love of California was clearly extolled more than once as several proud Texas cowboy sales clerks tried to entice her into wearing a western style blouse and one remarked, "Well, you're in the West now, Ma'am." Her defiant direct comeback, "Well I come from California. You can't get any further 'West' than that. Now can you?" left them nodding, tongue tied in agreement. Mom had no qualms, making it clear she didn't like the idea of changing herself to please the surrounding Texas locals. She was who she was and that was not a cowgirl. However she complied for dad's sake to dress us in cowboy attire and I was thrilled with my new wardrobe. I became the proud owner of a turquoise and white plaid, western shirt with pearl snaps, an engraved leather cowgirl belt with a terrific, shiny, western style buckle, as well as a very fine matching turquoise cowgirl hat with a matching satin ribbon.

Every woman remembers her very first pair of Levi jeans and how they felt. Mine were fittingly obtained in Houston, Texas. Dad donned his Stetson over his now white-gray, flat top, crew cut hair, his bright blue eyes shining below the brim. He looked very dapper in his new cowboy attire. He sported a bright white, western shirt with pearl snaps and a black cowboy string tie, pulled up taut at the collar just under his chin displaying a shiny, silver Brahma bull horned slide. My brother was his carbon copy and looked just as sharp in his black cowboy hat and western string tie. Mom was western wear non-conforming but looked lovely in a shapely pale, blue cotton dress with 3/4 sleeves, crinoline lined full skirt, wide tightly belted waist, short white gloves, white patent leather handbag on her arm and freshly polished, white, pointy, high heels. The Martin A. Byrnes, Jr., NASA family was ready to roll in our western wear in an open air convertible down the main streets of downtown Houston. We were thrust into the rodeo fanfare as the city and state happily embraced NASA, appreciative of the increased revenue and attention the space program would bring. On this particular day we, the Byrnes family, were the face of NASA.

Sandwiched between horses and marching bands we were slowly driven down the city streets of Houston with cheering crowds rubber necking, gaping back at us. I gazed up at high rise buildings dwarfing us while seated in the convertible back seat with my family, my blonde hair peeking out from under my turquoise cowboy hat following dad's direction to wave and smile big at the crowd just like a little junior Miss America. The wave and smile came naturally for dad, his big jovial smile lighting up the crowd as he humbly waved back, saying hello, many people wanting to shake his hand. He was humble, took it all in stride, shaking his head in disbelief with his typical rolling laugh. He knew they were not really there for him but for NASA and the astronauts. They were the real stars; he was their representative. He had been to Houston many times paving the way, meeting the mayor and city officials, working out the details to move NASA to Houston, helping to create NASA's main headquarters as the country embarked on the "Final Frontier."

The parade route ended, we disembarked the open convertible car and entered the giant stadium for my first ever western, cowboy rodeo. The unequivocal and distinct excitement in the air was enthralling and hypnotizing. Our little family moved forward, walking together, hand in hand with dad at the lead along with the crushing flow of the crowd.

Gawking up at large affable men in big cowboy hats with lit cigars hanging from their mouths, I watched as they exuberantly greeted dad with "Howdy Partner" and referred to mom as "the little woman", a term my mother clearly did not enjoy; however, they were oblivious as she feigned a polite smile standing next to and supporting my father.

My brother and I were dwarfed by the adults, swept along with the massive flow, cowboy suits everywhere around us, no other children in sight. My eye level view afforded a plethora of alligator cowboy boots and large, shiny western belt buckles, crushing in, surrounding me from all sides, relentlessly pressing me along. Caught up in the cowboy stampede, I grasped tightly to mom's hand and she to mine as the thunderous, southern drawl of cowboy greetings floated overhead accompanied by festive, macho back slapping and exuberant hand shaking. The familiar smell of horses pulled me eagerly forward until finally the dirt floor of the rodeo arena came into view.

We were guided to our seats in a VIP box section just above the arena dirt floor, very near the shoots where the bulls were released. I was enraptured by the smell of cows and horses in the air, simply thrilled as I watched several spectacular, sleek, muscular horses appear. A top each horse perched on fine leather saddles sat straight-backed, beautiful cowgirls in short, patriotic, fringed, cowgirl skirts. Exuding bright, ruby red smiles they proudly pranced in a circle around the arena each firmly holding tall flag poles. The Texas and U.S. flags proudly flying in the breeze as they rode.

Then the action really began. Simply astonished, I sat bug eyed as swift cowboys donned skillful, snorting horses which shot out of corral gates. Like lightening they jumped off the horses while still moving and wrestled cows to the ground tying their hooves in record times. Bells rang and there was much applause as the announcer gave the fastest time. Then my eyes fixed on the largest animals I'd ever seen, the Texas Brahma Bull. Dad had told us about these mighty bulls but nothing could have prepared me for this amazing up close, personal view. Brave, range-worn, agile cowboys climbed into the pen with the huge, fire-eyed bulls as their horns loudly, defiantly slammed into the gates protesting their confinement. The stadium seemed to breathe in all at once in silent anticipation then the doors of the shoot suddenly flung open. The giant beasts exploded from the shoot, cowboys skillfully held on for dear life as they spasmodically attempted to ride them one after another only to be thrown every time. I jumped from my seat several times with my mouth hanging wide open in amazement as I watched cowboys and hats flying into the air in all directions inevitably, unavoidably landing hard before us with a thud on the dirt floor, surrounded by a cloud of dust each time. Astonished I wondered why anyone would ever attempt such a thing.

Cowboy clowns bravely ran out performing funny shenanigans to distract the devilish, snorting beasts while the cowboys drug themselves up off the dirt to run for safety and wave to the crowd. It was euphoric and intoxicating. I was completely enthralled with Texas.

Mom's heart might have still been in California but for me there was no doubt ... I was home.

Chapter 2

Glen Valley Avenue

Our arrival in Texas was a roller coaster of ups and downs. The ecstatic emotional high of the rodeo, cowboy world contrasted at first with the family everyday life. We lived for a brief, lonely time in the Franklin Luxury Apartments. We were still not enrolled in school, waiting for a decision on a new home to definitively know which Catholic school we would attend. Here a few winter months felt like years, during the process of choosing a brand new three bedroom home which was much bigger than we were accustomed to. Although days drug on at the apartment, it wasn't long before our family moved into a brand new suburban ranch style home on Glen Valley Avenue, situated at the very end of the street. Just like in Lancaster, there were inviting adventurous vacant fields behind and on the left of us that seemed to stretch forever. Just a short bike ride and within view out over the vacant field lay Houston's International Airport at the time, now named Hobby Airport. Occasional bike rides to the airport afforded random celebrity sightings of famous stars like Jerry Lewis and Fess Parker.

Clearly we had come up in the world with my father's standing at NASA. No more rentals; we were buying a house this time, a home of our own, which gave us a feeling of permanency. The metal dinette table with red, vinyl covered chairs was retired as this home came with a cozy, breakfast nook comfortably fitting a family of four which also called for a smaller, updated dinette. In the center of the nook over the table hung a copper-hood light fixture which gave off a warm yellow glow.

In this home we gathered mostly in the comfort of the large Maple wood paneled den and TV room which had a fun, shuttered, pass-through window from the kitchen to the den with a view of the TV, where mom would stand and prepare dinner or wash the dishes while still watching TV. It felt like such stylish luxury then. Also this house gave us added space with a separate living room and formal dining room which required new, sleek, modern '60s furniture for visitors and special occasions. I was allowed to play with my Barbies in the empty living room space until the new furniture arrived. Mom had ordered an all white, over stuffed tapestry couch and sleek modern walnut coffee table and side tables along with two tangerine, tapestry covered occasional chairs. The first week of the couch's arrival, I took my homework into the living room to enjoy the comfort of the new couch.

In those days all the school children used fountain pens with permanent blue liquid ink, similar to the old ink well version but with refillable cartridges. I set my pen down while I studied my school book, researching an answer and when I turned to pick it up it had leaked a giant blue ink stain all over mom's brand new white couch cushion. There was no hiding it and, needless to say, after loud disappointed cries, much scrubbing of the stain and many tears, the living room became off limits except for special occasions and the yearly Christmas tree.

Also an absolute luxury for us was the double two car garage with two sectional, sliding garage doors which would become the scene for several of my childhood plays that never quite got off the ground. My room had a stylish bay window and window seat which I loved. When the curtains were drawn it made a great hiding place filled with pillows and stuffed animals. Many Wrigley chewing gum wrappers were folded and chains were constructed in this window seat as well as many hours of diary writing.

Comfortable decorative used brick adorned the front of our one story house. In this neighborhood, the front yard of each ranch style home came adorned with a glass, gas pole-light and a shadow box, cedar, slat fence enclosed the backyard. Dad planted a wonderful double trunk birch tree in the center front yard next to the gas light melding warm memories of Virginia to Texas.

The mortgage payment for this brand new three bedroom beauty in 1960 was $160 a month, the gas light bill $1.50 per month. It burned day and night as long as the mantles were working. I was encouraged by dad to plant a Marigold garden and we chose a spot in the backyard against the far fence just beyond mom's clothesline and went to work. Dad shoveled and turned the dirt preparing the stretch of ground for planting. Together we placed bricks around its edge and then I planted the seeds, watering daily waiting for growth; however in Texas the clay bound ground eked out pitifully puny flower sprouts so my interest waned quickly. Dad, mom and I discussed planting the front door brick planter with Boxwood bushes and mom's favorite Holly bushes, which at Christmas time promised bright red Holly berries. We had much fun decorating and picking out flooring, carpet, curtains and, much to my delight, new bedroom furniture.

S&H Green stamps were the rage for many years through the '60s. So with each grocery shopping trip we collected sheets of stamps to fill Green

Stamp books. I spent many hours sitting at the table in the breakfast nook, licking away at stamps or patting them with a little sponge, pasting them into stamp books, all the while looking through the S&H Green Stamp catalog with mom making our S&H wish list. We usually made our visits to the store to trade our stamps for goodies on Bonus Stamp Days where they would increase in value. Many accessories and occasional tables were attained via the Green Stamp store.

My parents were faithful to enroll us in private, parochial school at St. Christopher's where I quickly learned that in Texas football was the #1 sport bolstered by a contagious, giant, sport spirit. Football spirit reached its pinnacle in the winter when we bundled up with our plaid lap blankets and thermos of hot chocolate when our family was invited to attend the Texas Aggie college football game at Rice Stadium. Sitting in the brisk cold cheering en masse while football teams waged war below to thunderous applause and cheers was invigoratingly captivating.

Shyness finally was overcome in Houston where I made friends easily. My demure quiet demeanor now blossomed into a gregarious, popular and effervescent preteen. The years of quiet introversion suddenly morphed into a social butterfly. It was a thrill when the boys would give the girls glittery, gigantic, football, mum corsages with long ribbons in the green and white school colors. I managed to receive several which were proudly pinned up to dry on the bulletin boards that dad framed, painted and hung in my bedroom. We rode horses, attended football games and parties, created group sets of Wrigley 20 foot, chewing-gum, zigzag chains, played volleyball, went bike riding, hiking, swimming, hung out at the mall, attended many school functions and practiced cheers for unofficial cheer leading squads. Official cheerleaders in those days were only voted on and chosen in High School. So in elementary school, as there were no junior high schools in those days, we only dreamt of being chosen for cheer squads and practiced for the future by creating makeshift cheer squads of our own. Much time was spent researching the school colors and cheer squad uniforms of the future Catholic High Schools as well as learning their cheers.

Our family doctor, Dr. West's family went to our church and his children to our school. Dr. West's middle daughter and I hit it off as she was a fun, athletic, tomboy type who loved to ride horses. There were many visits to her house which was a sprawling Texas ranch where we were free to ride the horses for hours. Here I was completely in my element.

There was a vernacular in Texas that Dennis and I quickly embraced as we blended into our surroundings with our new fellow compadres. A Texas accent quickly enveloped my verbiage. "Yes ma'am, No ma'am, Yes sir, No sir and Ya'll" rolled off my tongue in an impressive Texas southern drawl as I adapted to my new home. I was fascinated to learn while out exploring on long walks with school friends after rainy days that tiny creatures looking like miniature lobsters, Cray Fish, would crawl up out of the sewer drains into the streets from the local bayou, which in Texas is pronounced 'bah-o' not 'bye-you.' I was only corrected by friends a few times to perfect that pronunciation. It was like a new language. I loved it, adapting quickly.

The highlight of every school year for me was when the nuns and priests would gather all the children in the gym to show NASA promotional and educational films. Dad would bring the film reels in steel gray, flat, round, tin cans, wind the film through the projector just so, then say, "Ok. Hit the lights." The school projector would begin to whirr and tick along and all the children including myself would be mesmerized by the images on the large portable screen at the front of the room. Complements of NASA and dad, we would sit quietly engaged treated to images of rocket booster launches, simulations and astronauts training for space travel. These films were cutting edge and high new adventure at the time. My brother and I were a big hit at our new school thanks to movie days. Also Dad's intro speeches where he made everyone laugh, including the nuns and priests also placed us in good stead.

As a result of my dad's standing in the church (having gone to seminary) and his NASA influence, much to my chagrin, the priests gave me extra special attention in catechism class. The young, slicked back, dark haired, dapper priest sporting a walking cane seemed to know who I was without an introduction. The first time I met him he entered the classroom nonchalantly then turned with a snap, pointed his cane directly at me, calling me out in the class, "And how are YOU doing today Miss Byrnes?" I jumped in my seat from nerves, squeaking out, "Fine, thank you, Father" and shrunk down into my desk. Once a week, the priest would arrive in class for a pop quiz. For the most part I overcame my shyness to share the correct answer with encouragement and special attention from the priest and learned very early on a big winning smile would always sway the priests my way. That, however, did not work quite so well with the nuns. I had developed a proclivity for much of my father's entertaining personality traits. My new-found acceptance and attention brought out a talkative, comedic quality better known as the preteen mouth. This was the conduit to trouble many times both at home and at school. I could always cause an unruly stir of laughter and boisterousness in a group of otherwise well behaved kids, which the nuns frowned on; however, I usually would avoid severe punishment because of my sweet angelic looks.

A deep fascinating admiration and fondness for the art of teased hair developed for me in the sixth grade. An absolute requirement for this process were massive amounts of Aqua Net hair spray, hair teased up in mounds – the higher the better, with tiny colorful bows placed just so on the side or center of the bangs. As a result of this bygone skill I still love the smell of Aqua Net to this day.

Many times Sister Catherine Marie would have to hunt me down as I gravitated to the mirrors with the older girls on break from the eighth grade classroom, who had gathered in the girls bathroom to primp, tease their hair, chew gum and joke around. They were pushing the envelope by chewing gum at school and I was pushing the envelope hanging out with them although I was gum free. This was a very early push toward the rebel in me. In those days, chewing gum at school was a huge rule breaker as were black patent leather shoes worn with skirts. Apparently a very imaginative nun or priest, at some point, decided that the black patent leather afforded the boys a mirror effect of the panties under the little girl's skirt. As hard as we tried we could never see what they were referring to but would never cross one of the stern nun's rules. Depending on the degree of misbehavior the result could likely end in being drug by the ear to the principal's office, being sent home for a whipping or a sharp rap across the knuckles with a ruler. Shudders of fear ran through me at the sight of the stern, never smiling nun who was our principal and Mother Superior creating a healthy fear to follow the rules. However, on this day our giggles and laughter in the bathroom could be heard down the hall into classrooms.

My claim to fame this school year was that just by sharing my new found gregarious nature I could turn sweet Sister Catherine Marie's face bright red. Patience exhausted, she would leave the other children at their classroom desks, fly down the hall, fling open the bathroom door with a whoosh, stand hands on hips, feet firmly planted in her well worn, highly polished, black lace up the front, nun shoes, propping the door open with one foot, rosary beads swinging madly from the waist of her long, black habit, whip her black and white veil over her shoulder as she glared at me pointing out the door of the bathroom and down the hall. Her words loudly echoed off the walls, "Elizabeth Ann Byrnes, what do you think you are doing? You get back in the classroom this minute... before I call your Mother and Father!"

The girls would ditch their chewing gum. I'd clamp my mouth shut, realizing I had crossed the line and scurry tail between my legs out the door and back down the hall into the classroom where all eyes were on me as I slid into the seat of my desk. All the classrooms could hear her scolding me. My brother who was in class directly across from the girls bathroom took heat from the children in his room about his rowdy, little sister causing trouble. He sloughed it off with, "Awwhhh she's always like that." I would forget about it as soon as I refocused on my school work and when the other children, especially a boy I really liked, Greg, asked me, "Are you okay?" I retorted, "Huh? Sure. It was nothin'."

The truth was Sister Catherine Marie was a sweet and wonderfully kind, compassionate person I admired greatly who loved all the school children like her own. To this day she is the one teacher who influenced me more than all others. Her high energy and loving spirit inspired me to be better and I hated when she wasn't pleased with me. Her love of English was contagious. She gave me the most treasured, beautiful gift as words came alive for me when she read books out loud to the class, her expressive voice rising and falling just in the right places. If the children enjoyed the book she would set aside other lessons to continue reading to us, a practice I also adhered to when home schooling my own children. Her infectious love of literature touched my artist heart as she taught me the joy of reading, movies and art. She inspired me and enriched my life, teaching me for the first time I was capable of more by placing me in advanced reading classes several years beyond my grade level where I read the classics: Stephen Crane's; Red Badge of Courage, Shakespeare's; Othello and Charles Dickens'; A Tale of Two Cities. She cared about us, nurtured and encouraged open thinking and sharing.

Our church and school boasted a small but beautiful old cathedral type church with intricate stained glass windows. It seemed so huge to me as a child. Here at St. Christopher's, the nuns expected us to sing our part in the children's church choir. On assigned Sundays, we would line up single file outside and ceremoniously head up the winding stairs to the choir loft, dressed in our Catholic school uniforms to sing the Latin responses at Mass for the priest. I attempted to follow in my dad's footsteps quickly finding, although I deeply loved music and quickly learned Latin, I did not have his singing musicality. The nun who led the choir was not an inspired teacher as was Sister Catherine Marie, which also made choir a punitive endured process rather than the making of a joyful noise unto the Lord.

On Sundays when I did not have to wear my uniform for choir, mom and I wore our netted pill box or bucket hats or lace scarves to Mass. Mom always looked wonderful and elegant in her A-cut beaver coat or mink capes, hats and gloves, her handbag on the crook of her arm, prayer missal in her gloved hand.

My brother was now an altar boy and looked very important in his altar boy frock, kneeling on the stairs of the altar during Mass. I always pensively watched with bated breath to see him ring the altar bells just at the right moments during the Consecration. Although he was a rowdy, rambunctious boy outside of church giving and receiving his share of hard knocks and black eyes, he always proudly performed his altar boy tasks perfectly. When he wasn't serving Mass, we would file in as a family down the main isle, genuflect, make the sign of the cross before the altar and take our pew seats right up front a few rows back from the altar near the right vestibule, where the sun hitting the stained glass windows bathed us in heavenly multi-colored light during Mass. I'd study those beautiful, intricate, Bible story, stained glass windows during Mass when the priest's fiery sermons drug on. On Dad's assigned days he would again sing the Mass. His enchanting Irish, tenor voice would echo through the intricate vaulted ceiling arches and church vestibules. I'd sit next to mom watching her listen with her head bowed in prayer, rosary beads in hand, her lips barely moving as she prayed the rosary while dad sang. I loved seeing and hearing Dad on the pulpit at Mass. In these moments my heart was full, so proud to be an Irish Catholic Byrnes.

Once a year, the school children highly anticipated the fun-filled church carnival held to raise money for the Knights of Columbus, a Catholic fraternal organization dad was a participating member of and actively supported all his adult life. Ferris wheels, games and rides magically appeared on the football field.

Mothers made tall frosted cakes for the musical Cake Walk. Darts, baseballs and rings were thrown and tossed to win prizes of stuffed animals, baked goods, homemade crocheted items and live gold fish. We all munched on barbecue, cotton candy and snow cones. Beer always flowed freely for the grownups at these carnivals. The church Barbecue was an all day and night affair. Many late nights were spent cleaning up and counting the money collected while children were tucked in safely at home with their latest stuffed animal prize snuggled next to them. Every year the Carnival was great fun and a monetary success for the church.

Chapter 3

Ginger

The 'local mall' was a wonderful new shopping experience which appeared in the '60s, a boon and magnet for teenagers but sadly the beginning of the end to mom and pop stores. They were a conglomeration of many stores in one place connected by one main walk way, usually two stories with escalators, but not yet covered under one roof as most malls are today. Many hours were spent at the 'Gulfgate Mall' record store while mom shopped at Joskes, Broadway, Levys or May Company department stores. The record stores had little rooms with glass windows and record players where you could sit behind closed glass doors and play all the newly released 45 records. We always gravitated to these rooms and monopolized them for hours chewing gum, singing along and bopping to the latest hits, spending our allowance on 45s to take home, to add to the stacks and play on our own stereo record players.

One gray winter evening on a visit to the mall, my mission was to buy mom a birthday present. My friend, Mary Beth, who always made me laugh, and her mother gave me a lift as they had shopping to do as well. Mary Beth's mother and I discussed and browsed for a present for mom which I could afford. Walgreens was a Texas drug store chain at the time complete with a soda fountain counter and pet shop. Here in the Walgreens pet shop I simply could not resist, I just fell in love with a cute little beige and white ball of puppy fur. Mary Beth's mother sounded doubtful as she quizzed me asking whether my mother wanted a dog for her birthday. I assured her, "Oh! Yes she does!" Impetuously, I decided to buy the little mutt, the runt of the litter with a crooked tail, a cute little bundle of fur for a whopping $1.06. Giggling and cooing, I lovingly held her in my arms and timidly took her home secretly afraid of my mother's reaction.

Dad roared with laughter when he saw the puppy and, begrudgingly, mom could not say no to her wiggly, little, cold nosed, birthday surprise. She tried to hide her smile as she retrieved a large box from the garage along with towels to set up a make shift doggy bed in the den, signifying the warm bundle had a new home. As dad examined the puppy he laughed as he noticed the tail declaring, "The six cents must have been for the crooked tail!" I asked mom to name her; she softened, assigning that job to me.

The snuggly, soft puppy was christened "Ginger" for her warm brown ginger color and soon my whole family came to love her, especially mom. I spent many long, loving hours confiding my deepest thoughts and feelings to Ginger, teaching her an array of tricks. Ginger showed her gratitude and love for me by obediently displaying her skill at shaking hands, sitting, laying down, rolling over on command and coming when called. She adeptly sat and stayed for extended periods in the middle of the backyard while I came inside to watch her through the den sliding door; then would run to me when I finally clapped and said, "Here girl" through the glass. Her crowning glory was that she could 'smile' and bark on command and balance a potato chip or doggy cookie on her nose then eat it on command, bouncing it from her nose into her mouth in one fell swoop without dropping it on the floor.

Ginger was also mom's faithful, loving, walking partner for many, many years long after I moved out of the house. One harrowing time, she escaped the confines of our shadow fenced yard to enjoy the pleasure of wallowing in the neighbor's newly fertilized and watered rose garden. The scowling neighbor drug her by the collar over to our house, banged on our front door, irate about her demolished garden, demanding restoration. Mom, too, was very upset her garden was spoiled and I was immediately given responsibility of cleaning it up and handed a shovel. Ginger was banned to the back yard with threats of the pound voiced and chained to a stake for punishment until she could be bathed. I begrudgingly complied working in the neighbor's yard, shoveling dirt back into place, muttering to myself, indignant she rebuffed both me and my pet so harshly. After all don't all dogs dig? Ginger was just playing, as far as I was concerned, and from my stand point her garden didn't look much different before or after the dirt was replaced. By the time I finished shoveling and repairing the dog digging damage, I was feeling very protective of Ginger. Memories of my little dog in Lancaster being shipped off by the dog catcher to the pound loomed heavily as I knocked on the door, told her I was finished, dropped the shovel and ran back home in tears, packed a bag and snuck Ginger off the tie down so she could not be taken away.

We ran away together, of course, no plan in mind but we were together. I found us shelter in empty new home construction down the street and resolved we would stay the night there and then decide what would come next. We sat together, alone on the concrete floor surrounded by the skeletal framing of an unfinished home, me crying with Ginger's nose sympathetically laying on my leg. It began to get cold and dark, dinner was waiting at home, shivers set in, shadows became long and noises scary so we walked on home. Mom asked where we had been and I said, "Oh, nowhere." Unbeknownst to me, she had secretly watched me pack my bag and take Ginger. She had let us go. I washed up for dinner and set the table. Life was back to normal. The incident was over, Ginger and I were home warm and safe. The neighbor continued to give both me and Ginger the evil eye when she saw us out on walks and I gave them right back. My loyalty and love for Ginger ran deep, the feeling was reciprocated.

Around the same time as the first Titan Rocket Launch in 1961 at Cape Canaveral, many of our familiar NACA and NASA families and friends had reunited, sifting in, moving to Houston for reassignments, preparing for the official opening of the NASA Space Research Center in September of 1963. Several had moved into our neighborhood. There were many cocktail parties and celebrations, including a city fashion show and luncheon which coincided with the Titan Launch, where mother was honored and given a beautiful ornate silver serving dish which I still have today.

This era in Houston was a wonderful, nebulous, euphoric place in time with a constant underlying feeling of celebration – a heady time for all. Many of the astronauts and their families had moved to an elite housing area near Houston called Clear Lake. All seven received corvettes each picking their own color and amenities. The seven original astronauts were the 'Rock Stars' of the day. I was as infatuated with them as everyone else. Dad supplied me with their pictures which I hung in my room along with my many horse statues and a large collection of stuffed animals. I knew the name of each astronaut and many details about their lives. I had my favorites. To me Wally Schirra was the most handsome and I was simply elated, jumping around the house, when dad came home and announced to the family that amiable Alan Shepard, who reminded me of my dad, was selected to fly into space first. Dad shared he would fly in the Freedom 7 capsule and would be the first American in space on May 5, 1961. I loved all the names of the Mercury capsules, waiting anxiously for Dad to reveal each new name. They all had a ring of patriotism and established history to them which melded so well with the exploration of the "Final Frontier."

Although Alan Shepard did not orbit the earth on his first flight into space he did eventually, ten years later, become the oldest astronaut, at the age of 47, to command Apollo 14, achieving the most accurate Apollo landing on record. He was a kind, fun loving, unassuming man and, to his credit, he also holds the place in history of the fifth person and the only Mercury astronaut to walk on the moon. Dad laughed when true to his fun loving character during this mission he hit two golf balls on the lunar surface. For this particular first space flight, however, he was blazing heavenly paths.

After Alan Shepard's first Mercury flight, he was greeted by a phone call from President Kennedy onboard The Champlain carrier. Then, upon returning home from sea to the U.S., he was given the first of many Mercury astronaut hero's welcome parades. These first flights however were a very nervous, anxious and exciting adventure for both the astronauts, NASA employees and their families. I begged for and heard stories from dad at home about fun and exciting times. They were not just his co-workers, they were also his friends. One such story was when Dad had been given an award from the new Governor of Texas, John Connally, appointing him "Admiral of the Texas Navy." Dad thought this was hilarious, as did all his friends. The astronauts, especially Gus Grissom, Alan Shepard and Wally Schirra, joked with dad about this many times and fondly anointed Dad, 'The Admiral'.

Deke Slayton arranged to give a signed picture of all sixteen of the astronauts, both the first and second teams, addressed 'To The Admiral'. Gus gave him a special rocket launch picture of Gus Grissom's Mercury, Freedom Bell 7, space flight to remember his flight. He was also honored to receive a very special Mercury plaque with a cut piece of a Mercury capsule heat shield stating, "To The Admiral In Recognition Of His Untiring Efforts Toward The Manned Space Flight Program For A Job Well Done."

Chapter 4

Kennedy Space Speech

In our home and lives, the space race had long been the central theme when President John F. Kennedy officially announced at Rice Stadium on May 25,1961 that the U.S. would put a man on the moon in three years. The day... the moment... of that speech was commemorated for all time for my family as dad sat only three rows behind the president. President Kennedy was my father's lifetime... my parent's lifetime... favorite president. Of course the fact that he was the first Irish, Catholic, Democratic president came up many times over in our household. There, on that day, President John F. Kennedy stood before the world and spoke of my father's dream, expressed his heart, to put man on the moon. Dad sat behind the president and in his brilliant blue eyes even on the black & white film of the day you can see the earnest personal fulfillment of this commitment. There is no doubt in his face or in his eyes that he is visualizing the success of man landing and walking on the moon. Dad saw it completed long before the astronauts ever entered space. For my dad, just as it was for all the other brilliant men and women who comprised NASA at the time, it was just a matter of continuing the work already in process. As dad looked at President Kennedy and then out to the distant sky and on up to the moon, his face, his eyes said it all.

This day was never spoken of in our house. The fact that dad attended the Kennedy Space Speech, met and spent time with, worked with President Kennedy, was never spoken of. For my dad it was his job, a job that needed to be completed for his country.

It was many years later, many years after dad had passed away, in 1994, as I home schooled my youngest two children, I discovered that my father had worked closely in Washington D.C. at the NASA Headquarters to achieve Kennedy's space mission. There he endeavored with the NASA team beginning stages of space flight, which inevitably brought to fruition, before the set target date, the achievement of the first U.S. man to step foot on the moon. I had just loaded a floppy disc onto our home computer which contained astronaut Buzz Aldrin's Space software. By this time in the '90s, almost every household had a personal DOS home computer. I loaded it randomly choosing the "Kennedy Space Speech" as something of interest for my youngest to share some family history and fuel my son's love of space. President Kennedy appeared in black and white on the monitor. JFK began speaking and there much to my utter amazement and shock, only rows behind the president's podium, sat my father just stage right and very fittingly under the American flag. The designers of the software kept the black and white true-to-the-era picture and eerily had frozen all the members in the audience except my father. I sat there stunned as Dad became animated and began movement with the president's words. First, leaning forward, carefully placing the day's agenda and papers in his hands on the floor under his chair, wiping the sweat from his forehead with his handkerchief on the incredibly hot, humid Texas day, then looking up at the president. As the president's words fell on his ears, he lifted his head, his eyes moving up and out to the heavens and then directly into my eyes through the screen. In that moment, you could see his spirit, his love of flight, his heart for travel to new frontiers, his boyhood lifelong dream of flying in his eyes. I looked into my father's animated, moving face and deep into his eyes and jumped out of my skin, flying up out of my chair as if he had come back to life right before me, screaming and pointing back at the computer, saying over and over, "It's Grandpa! It's... it's... IT'S DAD! IT'S DAD!" The children and my husband gave me looks which clearly questioned my sanity, my stuttering, stupefied response eliciting very puzzled reactions.

When I finally calmed down enough to explain they also viewed the screen, ultimately coming to learn and know who their grandfather truly was. Later in 1998, the mini series 'From The Earth To The Moon' premiered on HBO and, much to my joyful surprise, there again was dad. The intro to each show played the same cut from the Kennedy Space Speech with my father just behind the president looking out to space sharing the same heart, the same quest as President Kennedy, the same moment in history. In his face and in his eyes, the wish fulfilled... man on the moon... mission complete.

Just as it had been at NACA, Dad wore many figurative hats at NASA in the early days; if it needed getting done he was the man. His first official title was Financial Management Officer and Personnel Officer. He over saw and assigned those below him to recruit and hire staff as NASA began to grow (the specific details at the time are listed at the back of the book in my father's memoirs).

The Center was growing and taking shape, however, Houston Space Center build duties abruptly segued to space flight recovery, as Dad was appointed to replace astronaut Wally Schirra as civilian liaison onboard the carrier, The Champlain, for all Mercury flights for the seagoing operations of the Mercury recovery force. All NASA civilians aboard Naval vessels of the recovery forces at sea reported to Marty Byrnes. He remained in this position, Logistics Manager for Space Flights, for all Mercury flights on all launch recovery carriers.

Along with the coordination of landing capsules at sea, one of his acting titles was Administrative Officer Of Mercury Cape Activities. One particularly dreaded but interesting assignment Dad found himself in was organizing the reporters for press conferences at Cape Canaveral, Houston and, especially, on board carrier ships during and after space flights. The press, journalists, reporters and photographers were kept separate from the crew and astronauts in their own special press room. It was Dad's job to keep them at bay for prepared press releases. After each space flight, it was required that the astronauts fresh from flight into space, first needed to go into a special contained sterile area for debriefing and debugging from 'space bugs' before meeting the press. The space craft required security and scrutiny after each space flight as well. Time was needed to study the effects of space on the human body and the space craft. No one at the time knew if there were dangers or how the human body would react to space travel. Space was a new frontier and all precautions were taken to ensure the safety of everyone and garner every bit of knowledge they could from each space flight before talking to the press. Everything was treated with highest security.

The media at the time was different as well. The majority were respectful and obliging journalists looking for the correct facts to share with the public-at-large and once dad set the rules in place they complied with no renegade reporters breaking the ranks to scoop stories. If they did, they were escorted from the ship and banned forever. That only happened once or twice on dad's command.

For the duration of every Mercury space launch and flight, dad spent time on board Naval carriers at sea for all ocean landings. He became acquainted with the Admirals and commanders of the carriers, some became good friends and, because of his position at NASA, he was given special onboard duties and privileges which required ship-to-ship visits. I was very excited when he brought home a picture of himself riding the Cherry Picker between vessels. My brother and I crowded in to see the picture he proudly and playfully displayed before us of himself as he sat in the kitchen breakfast nook after a space launch trip. Looking back at me from the picture was my dad smiling big while he sat in some sort of contraption. His jovial, warm laughter filled the room as he gathered us close to look. I sat on his knee while he explained how he was strapped into the basket of the 'Cherry Picker' and transported above ocean waters between carrier ships as they lined up side by side somewhere in the Atlantic off the coast of Florida. I had many questions for him, envious of the ride. He explained the Cherry Picker was a way of transferring sailors and supplies from one ship to another, utilizing a set of cables and pulleys connected to two Naval carriers. The sailors pulled the rolling basket across the cables, moving it through the air between ships. It was a slow, harrowing process, especially if the wind kicked up, waving the basket to and fro. Dad shared that gusts of wind were very strong the day he made this particular transfer. He was a good sport, looking like a big kid perched in the basket, a giant grin plastered on his face, yet the anxious look in his eyes betrayed his beaming childish grin as he nervously held on tight. He revealed to us he was extremely grateful to make it back safely to the deck of The Champlain. He assuaged our fears by stating it was a common way of transferring from ship to ship and that the service men would never allow anything to happen to him stating, as he patted my head, "No one has ever landed in the drink."

My first and only media experience growing up happened during the building of the NASA Center after the first buildings were erected. I was asked as the daughter of Martin Byrnes to do an interview for a local city magazine. Fixing my hair special in a bob with bangs, I fastened a little bow on the side, dressed in a blue pleated skirt, white cotton, princess-collared blouse tucked at the waist, navy cardigan sweater and black leather flats with white ankle socks. I hesitantly and shyly met the lady reporter and photographer, who first arrived at the house for a photo shoot in my room. They wanted to capture me with all the astronaut pictures. Then we drove to pick up another interviewee, a young boy a couple years older than me. I remember he was very talkative, much to the reporter's relief. We then traveled to the new NASA Center for another photo shoot in front of the newly installed NASA sign, which was ground level in front of the new main building. On the drive, they conducted the main interview in the car. Overall, it seemed like a couple of hours of questions, answers and photos. My shyness returned around strangers, making it a difficult interview. Although it was painful for me, I did give them many answers, however stilted or abrupt. Yet the printed story held many quotes from me that I did not say. The pictures were nice, for the gawky young girl I was, moreover I was very upset when I read what was written and realized the words printed were not my words. Angrily, I protested to my parents but what was done was done. Left with a bitter taste of the adult real world, I decided to forever swear off interviews, a decision that was amusingly never tested as no one ever again asked for one.

The new Princess light-up phone in my parent's bedroom became a lifeline tether to preteen life. Times were advancing and we now had two phones in the house, not just one. Sitting on my parent's bed gabbing endlessly with friends became my favorite past time. Party lines were fading out of existence and we could no longer eavesdrop on other people's calls, a favorite past time in Virginia. We could now dial straight through without the assistance of an operator. Area codes and pre-fixes were assigned across the country. I'd chat, stretched out for hours in my parents room, most of the time hair up in curlers, painstakingly set with Dippity Do, rolled up in large brush curlers, held in place with pink plastic spikes then covered with the bouffant cap from the new hair dryer mom and I shared. The plastic, turquoise, portable, Sunbeam hairdryer with the matching turquoise, see through, nozzle hose connected to the base of the bouffant cap, which then pumped in hot air, afforded us dry, curly hair in about an hour instead of leaving curlers and pin curls in all day or night. It was a luxury and a freedom not to have to sleep in curlers all night. I'd chat on the phone with the receiver stuck under the cap attached to my ear as the dryer ran.

Polka dancing with dad was replaced with dancing in the den to Chubby Checker's Twist and Del Shannon's Run, Run Runaway, the number one hit on the charts in the U.S. Just around the same time Del Shannon first appeared on Dick Clark's American Bandstand, astronaut Alan Shepard became the first U.S. man in space on May 5, 1961. Harmoniously for me, Del Shannon, his stage name and Charles Westover, his given name, became a very good friend later in life. Sadly the world lost him too soon on Feb. 8, 1990. He was a wonderful, down to earth, talented musician and entertainer, a kind, caring and charismatic man.

Chapter 5

Out At Sea On Carriers

Dad was often sociable with most all the astronauts. He was especially fond of affable and friendly Virgil 'Gus' Grissom who was the second astronaut in space for a fifteen minute suborbital flight in the space capsule, Freedom Bell 7, July 21,1961. Enjoying a similar sense of humor they spent time in one another's company at the special NASA "watering hole" bar. It was no secret that pilots, astronauts and those who worked with them loved to party and drink. It was Gus Grissom who originally dubbed dad "The Admiral". Gus was the smallest astronaut. I remember dad affectionately laughing about the, 'Gusmobile', which was the name that was given to the Mercury capsule that was designed specifically for Gus that no other astronauts could fit into because it was too small. Dad shared humorous stories of Gus taking mementos of little rocks for friends into space with him, sneaking them onboard so his friends could say they had space rocks. I have wonderful memories of dad laughing, jokingly shaking his head divulging that when the capsule was unable to be retrieved by the helicopter at sea and sank it was 'probably' because of the silly 'space rocks' crazy Gus took on board which may have weighed it down too much for salvage.

The official statement, of course, was that the hatch blew too soon and the capsule flooded and sank. Eventually, the capsule was recovered in 1999 and NASA concluded that Gus had done nothing to cause the sinking of the capsule. I know that dad would have been very happy that Gus' legacy was finally cleared of all speculation. At the time of the capsule sinking, NASA families and the world sat with bated breath as Gus was harnessed successfully and then pulled up by ropes from the ocean waters to the safety of the helicopter. A collective sigh of relief spread throughout mission control and all the NASA family's homes and the U.S. as we sat glued to the TV. Then in horror we watched as the helicopter tried several times in vane to retrieve the capsule. It was just too heavy filled with ocean water. It sunk but not before it almost pulled the helicopter into the water seconds before finally being released. It was only recently in reading my father's unfinished memoirs I learned it was in-fact Dad who made the final call to let Freedom Bell 7 sink. He ascertained that everything of the greatest value had been retrieved, the astronaut was safely onboard the helicopter and headed to the carrier, the information had been sent to Mission Control and the water filled capsule was just too heavy for salvage and was dangerously on the verge of dragging the helicopter and crew under. He commanded, "Drop the capsule!" It was released to the ocean waters to sink. He then told the Captain to mark the area with a buoy flag so they would know the general area where the capsule sank. He then ran with the Captain to the Chart Room to peruse the maps of the ocean floor to ascertain where to recover it. There they discovered it had been dropped over the deepest part of the ocean floor which was over 5 miles deep. He was astonished to learn there simply was no way it could be recovered and had been lost for all time. They had no idea that in future years it would be salvaged by those who discovered the Titanic.

[Please read my Dad's memoirs at the back of the book for the harrowing description of this moment in history and memories of his dear friend Gus Grissom.]

Astronauts and most especially the early astronauts, the true pioneers, pushed the envelope against danger and death for the advancement of space travel. Years later, sadly, Gus did not escape as he sat on the launch pad at Cape Kennedy strapped into Apollo 1 for his third space flight. He died tragically on January 27, 1967 in an oxygen-fueled fire along with astronauts Ed White and Roger Chaffee, both friends of dad's as well. All three space heroes in our home. It was a harrowing, heartbreaking, devastatingly painful setback for NASA and all who loved them. The loss affected dad deeply. No one at that juncture had ever died in the pursuit of space flight. It was a huge wake up call for NASA and all involved.

John Glenn, to his credit the squeaky clean astronaut, who did not hang out at the same "watering hole" as dad or the rest, was chosen to become the first man to orbit the earth. We were enjoying the hilarious Harlem Globetrotter's crazy basketball games, the new to TV Flintstone cartoons along with Freddy Cannon's; Way Down Yonder In New Orleans and Neil Sedaka's; Calendar Girl on our transistor radios and record players as John Glenn prepared to become a national hero. I sat in the den with mom transfixed at the TV watching John Glenn fulfill his place in history as he boarded Mercury, Friendship 7 on February 20, 1962. The excitement was palpable as we listened to the count down from Mission Control and then watched the fiery, smoke filled 'lift off' from the rocket launchpad at the Cape, each launch always bringing us up off the couch to our feet. We listened and watched on pins and needles breathing a sigh of relief as each new tracking station placed strategically around the world acknowledged contact with him, waiting anxiously for his static reply back each time as he became the first man to orbit the earth. Then, we just as pensively watched as his space capsule successfully landed in the Atlantic, breathing another huge sigh of relief knowing dad was somewhere very close by and the capsule did not sink this time. However, he did bruise two knuckles when he blew the hatch at the end of his mission.

It was now May 19,1962 and the talk everywhere was about Marilyn Monroe singing Happy Birthday to the President at Madison Square Garden and my mother openly stated in disgust, "It's just disgraceful!" She was clearly not happy with her performance, while my dad seemed amused. I couldn't understand at the time why mom was so upset over such a glamourous Hollywood event. To me Marilyn, who was beautiful, just didn't really know how to sing very well. I thought, "Wow you would think they would get someone who can sing better for the president." Not understanding the connotations at the time, I just thought it all a rare curiosity. The nuns would not allow us to speak of it at school so we all whispered about in the girl's bathroom and at the football field bleachers after school. It wasn't until a little later in life her sexy solo, which had by then become an iconic tribute, made sense to me.

The space race continued and Scott Carpenter flew the second successful American manned orbital flight on May 24,1962 in Aurora 7 spacecraft. Each flight was a trip away for dad and each flight an exciting celebrated moment in history. This particular flight, Scotty, as dad called him, identified fireflies as 'frostflies', which were really frozen liquid drops surrounding the capsule. I always pictured these much like the fireflies we would catch in Virginia. He was also the first man to eat in space. It wasn't long after that mom bought us instant orange Tang, the official drink of astronauts and a staple in our kitchen for many years to come.

The same year in 1962 while we all danced the Mashed Potato and sang along with Bobby Vinton while we played the 45, Roses Are Red, on our family stereo record player, Wally Schirra prepared to launch into space. On October 3, 1962 Wally Schirra chose to prove a point in his friend, Gus Grissom's defense when he remained inside his spacecraft, Sigma 7, at the end of the longest orbital flight to date, a 6 orbit mission. Schirra forever my rebel, astronaut hero, insisted on bucking the system. Breaking protocol, the space capsule was scooped out of the ocean by the helicopter and deposited safely on the deck of the carrier with Schirra still implanted inside. Dad had to approve this move and it was his thought that if Schirra had a reason for this, although it wasn't protocol, then why not let him do it. When it was finally securely in place on deck, he purposely and deliberately made a point to hit the hatch hard with his fist to blow the hatch, also like Glenn, bruising his hand in the process.

I have memories of dad standing silent with the look of satisfied determination on his face as he watched, after the fact, as the news anchor talked about his friend's defensive, supportive actions which spoke louder than any words. All the astronauts were made of very tough stuff, however, Wally Schirra proved to be the one gruff Mercury astronaut who would fly on all three projects – Mercury flight, Sigma 7, then a successful Gemini 6A orbital flight with astronaut Jim Stafford on December 18, 1965.

This 6A launch got off to a rough start. At first, the booster rocket abruptly shutdown seconds after ignition, resulting in the launch being aborted. Again bucking the system, Schirra against protocol made the wise decision not to eject because he did not feel any upwards motion, which was the absolute correct call for the astronaut's safety. The flight then launched three days later. Wally displayed for the universe his sense of humor as he played Jingle Bells on a four hole Hohner harmonica he had smuggled onboard. Later, they would make a special version of this harmonica naming it after him. This comical universal musical prowess really made dad laugh. Then, Schirra felt strongly after safety improvements were made to the Command Module, he would follow in sequence after his friend Gus Grissom, where he flew a third time into space in the first successful, manned Apollo 7 flight which launched on October 11, 1968. Dad remained very good friends with Wally Schirra throughout his life.

My parents had ongoing parties and grand celebrations while my school friends took turns having monthly home parties. The Catholic church, defeating the purpose of the rule to prevent promiscuity, would not allow school dances, so we created our own at home. Large groups of preteens would excitedly gather at these parties, playing our music loud, dancing and much fun would ensue. We would lower the lights, preteens would pair off, couples retreated to dark corners or sat snuggling on the sofa in between chaperone checks. In these moments, boys would nervously put their arms around timid girls, first kisses were received and given with hot making out by some between parent's checking in on us, something that most assuredly would not have happened at a supervised school dance. Fun was had by all even the ones not kissing and making out. Everyone looked forward to these parties, all pitching in bringing their 45 records. We danced to Sweet Little Sheila and Duke of Earl to name just a couple. My absolute favorite were the Motown songs with the Supremes, Fats Domino, James Brown, The Drifters, The Coasters, along with Ray Charles. There were so many. Of course Roy Orbison, the Everly Brothers and Brenda Lee were my absolute favorites too. Johnny Angel by Shelley Fabares was my sixth grade theme song but the list goes on and on as I did indeed inherit my dad's love of music. Many times he would sing along with my records as I played them on the stereo in the den or on the radio in the car. I loved when I was alone in the car with dad and I could share my music with him. The American radio DJ became an entertaining staple and we had our favorite AM radio channels. FM radio channels were not yet available. We each had our own transistor radios and listened intently while the DJ's cranked out the tunes. Those portable little transistor radios were our constant companions much like cell phones or ipods are today. There were many a night after night time prayers I'd fall fast asleep listening to my transistor radio as it lay on my pillow. Mom or dad would come in to check on me and turn it off so as not to waste the battery. One single four volt battery is all it took.

Embarrassed and thrilled on my birthday mom plotted with my friends to throw me a surprise birthday party. I ran to dive for cover when all my friends leaped out screaming, "Happy Birthday, Betty!" as I walked in the front door wearing my metal braces retainer which looked like a horse harness. Awkwardly I ducked, hiding my head in utter mortification, scampering like a squirrel seeking escape, dodging and darting off to my room, avoiding a stream of friends hot on my trail asking me what was wrong. I sheepishly removed the harness and changed into nicer clothes, angry my mother made me wear my harness knowing full well everyone was showing up. Later, of course, I realized she didn't want me to have any clue or ruin the surprise sticking to the normal routine; however, it took me awhile to forgive her. It was a flattering rush and preteen dream come true until half way through the party my heart was completely crushed as I learned the boy I was madly in love with, Tommy Sudela, liked another girl at a different Catholic school.

My first love unrequited, I pictured some beautiful blonde girl much prettier than myself as rejection set in. The rest of the night I dramatically and tearfully played, "It's My Party and I'll Cry If I Want To" by Lesley Gore repeatedly, putting a real damper on the upbeat mood. At the request of some of my guests, Dad tried to step in and save the party but my heart was morosely broken. Finally, much to everyone's relief, it was time for the kids to disperse as parents arrived. I soon recovered but never got over my first heartbreak love. There were, thankfully, many more happy parties to come.

Ironically and interestingly Tommy Sudela took a great interest in me years later only weeks after I had married. He traveled from Texas to California unannounced, knocking on my parent's door looking for me only to be told by my mother that I had just been married. I never heard from him again. Some things maybe are just not meant to be.

In 1962 life was good for the Byrnes family in Houston. School was great. My brother and I both had many friends. He played football and the family attended his games each weekend. I practiced at cheerleading in an effort to make the squad at my chosen girl's high school and was quite adept at back bends and high toe jumps. We both were already planning ahead, setting goals, choosing which Catholic high schools we'd be attending. In those days, you went straight from elementary school, which went to eighth grade, then onto high school. My biggest joy and honor at the time was to receive the giant white football mum corsage from an admirer. Everyone was going steady and if you received a St. Christopher medal necklace from your boyfriend, a sign you were going 'steady,' then you were the envy of all the girls, a practice the Catholic church put a stop to some years later. Apparently St. Christopher was the saint of 'safe travel' not the saint of going steady, holding hands and making out under the bleachers or making it to second base in the gym.

Mom became a Girl Scout leader and embarrassed me thoroughly enforcing Girl Scout protocol. I was the only Girl Scout who refused to comply with Girl Scout rules, showing the first signs of the rebelliousness to come. I would sit through the meetings endlessly wishing instead to be hanging out on the football field with the boys. Much to my mother's dismay, after spending the money on the green uniform and painstakingly sewing on all the patches, I showed little interest in earning badges. I think mom thought if she was the leader she could corral my increasingly wild spirit. Although I was shy, I knew what I wanted and always marched to my own drummer which led to occasional problems, proving that quiet rivers run deep.

On days when we didn't wear our Girl Scout uniforms and we wore our regular Catholic school uniform, we were allowed to stay after to watch football practice. The girls sat in the bleachers doing our homework and sneaking peeks at the boys as the young, red headed Irish priest, who was the coach, ran them through their drills. We were a two-car family by now, so Dad would come after work to pick us up in his old Chevy clunker similar to the one we drove across country from Lancaster. My parents were still very frugal and used cars were always purchased. Dad thought this old Chevy was just the ticket. We'd run to the car, Dennis all sweaty and stinky from football and me just happy to see dad but embarrassed by the old car. We'd scramble in and I'd say, "Oh, Dad, why do you have to drive such an old, ugly car? It's embarrassing!" My brother would command, "Shut up Betty!" Dad would laugh and say, "You don't like my car? What's wrong with the old girl?" Arriving home to Ginger's cold nose, licks, wagging tail and a nice, hot dinner on TV trays in the den while we watched Mr. Ed and The Beverly Hillbillies on our console Motorola TV would complete the day.

Dad absolutely loved Johnny Carson who had just replaced Jack Paar on The Tonight Show and occasionally I'd get to stay up late on weekends to watch with him if mom and dad weren't out at a party. He'd laugh big belly laughs when, Bill Dana, would do his schtick. He was the comedian all the astronauts welcomed into their inner sanctum at the watering hole. He endeared himself to them all with his astronaut persona, José Jiménez, and became known as the eighth Mercury astronaut. Dad would laugh thunderous roars the minute he heard, "My name - José Jiménez." Bill would hang out at and party on many occasions with the astronauts and those from NASA.

Life was good.

Chapter 6

The Realty Of Fear

Shocking word came that there was someone who was threatening dad at work. As I stated earlier, dad wore many hats at NASA and one of those hats was Man Power Personnel or Human Relations, the hiring and firing of employees on the grounds at the NASA Center, Human Resources today. He had been given the thankless job of cutting those who could not fit the bill for the large task at hand... to complete the mission to the moon. He was put in a position where his job was to fire several men, telling us sullenly he felt very badly about it, trying to be kind, letting them go with dignity and compassion. He even personally found jobs for some; however, one man in particular who had been let go was blaming dad for his departure. He was very angry and dad was taking the brunt of this man's anger in the worst way. The fired employee physically came at him in his office attacking him and threatened to kill him and his family (swallow... that would be us). My parents were advised by NASA security and the Houston police to pack up and move to a motel where the man could not find us until they could locate and confine him. It had been reported he had a gun, so dad left work early and arrived home to head up the swift packing process to get us all to safety. We were told to move fast. We also needed to find someone to care for Ginger because we could not bring her with us. Mom arranged quickly for the lady down the street, Goldie, the wife of another NASA couple I really liked, who owned the big white, hard top Cadillac with huge fins to take her. I knew she was safe there in Goldie's yard.

We pulled out our familiar suitcases threw a few changes of clothes and items into them. Dad came to my room and with a nervous smile told me anxiously to take one of my favorite stuffed animals to hang on to and something to play with. I grabbed what was needed, took one last look at my room before we were shuffled out to the car for a long ride to Galveston where we stayed in a motel. We found a little place with a kitchenette so mom could fix us meals. She had brought some food along so we wouldn't have to go out and shop or be seen much. Dad ventured out to the store for a few items and was back quickly locking the door behind him. Dad and mom wanly attempted fun excitement to make it seem like we were just going on vacation, but it didn't feel like any vacation or trip we'd ever been on. We planted ourselves in a motel room on our non vacation, uprooted from our everyday life, no school, no friends and waited to hear if the police had found the man threatening our lives. We couldn't even go outside to play or swim in the motel pool, although it was too cold for swimming. We just waited, watching TV and trying to stay occupied.

During this time, if that was not scary enough, the Cuban Missile Crisis happened. It was 1962, we sat on the beds in the motel room gathered as a family watching the news on TV. I sat next to my dad with my arm through his, looked at him and mom and asked, "We don't have a bomb shelter. Are we going to die?" My dad reassured me, "No. No, Betty Ann. We will be fine. President Kennedy will take care of it." President Kennedy was launching mankind to the moon; he most certainly could take care of the Cuban dictator, Fidel Castro and communism invading the U.S. Our convictions were firm yet we nervously watched the news.

We were trapped in a motel room just like the ones we were so familiar with from our travels across country. All there was to do really was play cards or watch TV, unfortunately on every channel (there were only about 7 channels in those days) was news about the Cuban Missile Crisis. Many of the news casters were people dad had met and he would comment about them as they talked. He liked most of them and always had a short one liner to share about them which made us feel as if we knew them too. Somehow, it made it more comfortable but that was always Dad's way. Mom and Dad smiled and assured us we were fine but several times they retreated out the door to the motel patio to talk privately, finally, coming in turning off the TV to play Old Maid and Fish with us to get our minds on simpler, happier things.

Teaching us to rely on prayer, we knelt that night at the side of the motel bed and said the rosary together and prayed. This was a tradition in our family for many years. We would kneel at the side of my parent's bed as a family and say the rosary on a regular basis. My parents firmly believed in and practiced: "The family that prays together stays together." We would also include our personal prayers and this night we each prayed for President Kennedy and the country. The Crisis passed, thankfully, and all credit was given to President Kennedy. Just as dad had said, he brought the country through safely. He was truly a hero in our home.

The frightful angry man who had threatened us was also found within days and with great relief we put that behind us and safely returned home. Dad was given the choice to press charges but asked that instead he be taken somewhere for psychiatric help. I learned that all types of crises in life eventually pass, especially when the bond of family love brings you through together. Returning to our lovely home, very much relieved, I was very happy to see Ginger again, giving her big hugs, lavishing kisses and attention on her. She was thrilled to see us all, showing her love as her crooked tail ferociously wagged her body. I had fretted and worried about her missing us while we were gone. She faithfully taught me the joy of sweet reunions.

We also learned in Houston that we did not leave bitter cold weather behind in Virginia as the first freeze of the winter season set in. Very early in the morning, just after sunrise only a day or two after returning from the motel incident, I had just gotten out of bed. I heard an out of the ordinary, very loud, demanding knock at the front door. Still in my pajamas, I pulled on my soft pink, quilted, satin robe and tip toed to the door. Our front door had a diamond shaped clear window in the center at adult eye level and just as I turned the corner from the hall way to investigate the loud knocking, I saw the most hideous, horrific, monster face smashed up against the glass. Standing frozen in fear, I screamed a blood-curdling shriek, believing with all my might the evil man who had wanted to hurt us had returned to harm us. Screeching with all my lung power, "He's back! He's back!" My brother came bolting from his room first. He also froze, scared out of his pjs after peeking at the door. We both just stood shaking, hiding around the corner in the hallway just out of sight from the demanding knocker, neither of us able to move screaming, "DAD! MOM!" Dad was in the shower preparing for work and didn't hear our screams for help. Mom came frantically running from the backyard where she was dealing with wrapping pipes to prevent freezing to find Paul Anderson, a friend of my dad's, at the front door. He, as it turned out, was there to drive dad to work as they were car pooling that day and thought it would be funny to make a schmush face on the glass. We were relieved it was a nice family friend, but I was not laughing. Mom chided and scolded him like a misbehaving child, "For goodness sake, Paul, get in here. You scared the kids. What were you doing anyway? Now I'll have to wash that window." His prank had landed on a very nervous lot. I was angry that he would scare us so terribly and stomped my foot as I indignantly declared, "Don't EVER do that again, Mr. Anderson! You scared me to death!" Dad came out carrying his suit jacket, cleanly shaven, his flat top wet and combed up straight, dressed for work in his bright white, freshly ironed dress shirt and typical bow tie. He brought relative calmness to the situation as always, explaining we were all still very nervous from our ordeal. Poor Mr. Anderson who was a jovial, happy soul with no children of his own never even thought about how we might still be frightened or on edge and apologized over and over until mom finally shooed him and dad out of the house.

Chapter 7

Malt Shops and Fast Food

Occasionally my school friends and I would get up very early and ride our bikes into church for early weekday, 7:00a.m. Mass before school. Also, not unlike today at any given time, the kids from school would get together and cook up a plan for an adventure. Looking for some fun we would peddle our bikes into town to the malt shop, take the bus to the mall or downtown to Houston, something again which would never be safe to do in today's world at that young age. On one occasion we gathered as a small group of boys and girls traveling by bus into downtown Houston for the Houston Rodeo Parade. This time, I was participating in the parade from street level in the crowd. The big draw was Michael Landon the VIP guest for 1962. All I knew was that I just simply had to see him and his horse in person. It was an odd sensation standing on the corner in the crowd now waving and cheering. We stood on the corner calling his name. He obliged us by prancing his painted pony over to us to say hello. He was even more charismatic and gorgeous in person than I could have imagined, dressed as Little Joe in his Bonanza clothes, looking as if he just stepped out of the TV. We were mesmerized and star struck as Michael Landon took off his hat in true cowboy gentlemanly fashion, nodded to us saying, "Hello!" Showing off that gorgeous curly, dark mane of hair he smiled that whimsical, amused, bright white smile down at us from a top his beautiful horse. Until this point for me my dad had the most beautiful smile on earth. Now I was thoroughly convinced no one on earth could have a smile as beautiful as Michael Landon's. He was what every movie star should be. All the girls swooned over Michael Landon. Yet for me his horse was simply even more amazing, holding me captive as every muscle moved in rhythm to his rider. They were one as he held his head high neighing and whinnying for the crowd, expressing his absolute star quality as Michael waved his hat in the air at the crowd. Then he was gone leaving us with memories for a lifetime; we headed home together on the city bus.

Word was out there was a new sort of eating establishment called McDonald's. It was sort of like a drive-in but with 'fast food' where you could buy a hamburger for only 15 cents and take it to go. Mom was a stickler about preparing and feeding her family home cooked, nourishing food on a budget. She did not like eating out but her friends all told her they had eaten there, taken their children and for only 15 cents the hamburgers were, "Good!" She had to admit the price was right. So while dad was gone on carriers for a space launch, we took our very first trip to McDonald's Golden Arches for dinner. I was in heaven. You could even sit down inside by this time; however, mom would only agree to trying the food so we took it to go. She ordered us each a hamburger, fries and a soda. Eating in the car was not a normal thing in those days but on this occasion mom allowed us to try out our hamburgers and fries in the car. Dennis and I loved it; Mom not so much. The Golden Arches were no draw for her. She said, "This is no kind of decent meal. I can make a better hamburger than this at home on the barbque. This will never last."

Nourishing, home cooked food was the only way to go for her until in her ailing later years when I cared for her. She developed a love of the Carl's

Superstar with French fries which I brought her weekly. She looked very forward to her hamburger meal each week. Her eyes would light up when she saw me walk in with the bag of steaming food. It became a real treat for her. In the late 1960's she did, however, grow to indulge in Kentucky Fried Chicken once a month and on occasional Friday nights would allow us to enjoy take out Fish n' Chips with malt vinegar to honor the Friday meat abstinence for Fish Fridays, as was the Catholic religious custom.

For a time, several of my new friends and I would sneak over to the local malt shop to enjoy hanging out and devour chocolate shakes and French fries. The juke box was loud, the waitresses were fun, the older teenagers hanging out made us feel grown up. One day, a friend's older brother showed up with his motorcycle offering rides. My friend didn't hesitate to hop on the back with her brother for a spin around town. They took off making it look easy and fun. When they returned, he motioned for me to hop on the back. I was very afraid but held fast to my grownup bravado wanting to impress others with my motorcycle prowess. I'd never even seen a motorcycle up close let alone ridden one. I simply didn't have a clue how to get on, ride or sit on a motorcycle. Swallowing my fear, ramping up as much moxie as possible and feeling rather gutsy, I hopped on the back of the bike, wrapped my arms around his waist as I'd seen my friend do and held on tight. Dressed in the typical Bermuda shorts of the day I had no clue where to put my legs. He yelled something and off we roared. Racing away my leg landed hard on the hot exhaust pipe. I bit my lip wincing silently in pain and held on tight as he raced through the circular round-about where the malt shop was located, the longest, shortest most painful ride of my life. As soon as he pulled in, upon return, I jumped off, my leg burning and sizzling, the skin was literally bubbling, pain throbbing up my leg, giving me a sick feeling. The waitress came to check on me bringing me butter to slather on the burn saying, "That's a bad one, Hon." I sat holding the butter there gingerly for an hour or so, finally making my way home. I felt there was no way I could tell my mother for fear of getting in trouble, thinking I'd never be allowed to see my new, fun, wild friends again. Although it was a hot and humid summer for three days I wore long pants to hide the burn, sneaking butter out of the kitchen to put on my leg, hiding the pain. I learned from experience applying butter to a burn is an old wives tale and does not help heal a burn. Mom and Dad were getting the feeling something was up with me and finally Dad came to my room asking me what was wrong. I pulled my pant leg up revealing the severe, ugly burn. He immediately called mom in who gasped and went right into nursing mode to help clean it up. A huge weight falling off my shoulders, I sheepishly confessed the series of events leading up to the burn, completely relieved to finally have those who loved me care for my pain. The end result was a visit to Dr. West's office, a very long lasting preteen war scar, which today I still have and no future visits to the malt shop.

Chapter 8

Bullets Change Everything

Excitement was in the air. We had received word on the morning news. Sister Catherine Marie's exhilaration was bubbling over as she shared with the class that President Kennedy was coming to town. She cheerfully asked how many of us were going to be there to see him, to greet him and Mrs. Kennedy at the airport. I was simply euphoric, inviting all my friends over to the house as I lived very close to the airport where the President and the First Lady, Jacqueline Kennedy would arrive. Many times I'd ridden my bike to the airport to garner chance meetings with celebrities; this time, however, crowds were gathering on Broadway, the main street directly behind my house which led directly from the main airport to downtown Houston. All we had to do was take a short walk across the vacant field behind my house and we were there. So several of my friends arrived after school and we excitedly walked over across the field through the scrub brush and sand to Broadway, prattling away, giddy with excitement.

Crowds were gathered all along the edge of the road rubbernecking to get the best view. I discerned the best place to see the President and First Lady and to possibly even be seen by them was on the meridian grass island at the center of the divided two-way, four lane street. All traffic had been stopped both ways on the street for their arrival, so we easily crossed the normally busy street with no trepidation and no secret service interference. It was a different time unlike the security of today. We took up our lone post on the middle meridian with a clear view to the airport exit, freely standing on the green freshly-mown grass in the open, anxiously waiting. Before we knew it the open air, big finned Cadillac convertible carrying President Kennedy and the First Lady was right before us. There was no protection like the closed in, armored limousine the president now travels in. There they sat in clear view in the back seat only a few feet away cruising at a very slow speed so we could get a really good look at them. We all waved and cheered. They were simply the most stunning couple I'd ever laid eyes on. She was so elegant in her pill box hat and dark brown hair; he was so handsome in his suit and tie with his thick hair. They were our American royalty and there I was, waving at them... and there they were, waving back. It was surreal.

The president beamed at the crowd, looking my direction I was convinced he smiled directly at me. He waved a hearty, friendly wave while Jacqueline smiled a sweet smile, also waving to the crowd in return. They were amiably talking to one another as they sat perched on the white leather seats of the convertible, pointing out people in the crowd to one another as they waved. They seemed very happy. Then they were gone.

Astounded at my good fortune and walking on a cloud I was bursting to tell my dad when he came home from work. His eyes sparkled as I enthusiastically shared my experience, clamoring on about every detail. He patiently, attentively listened as I at first bounced around him excitedly then sat on his knee with his arm around my neck. He was thrilled for me and laughed his big belly laugh, tweaking my nose and hugging me as I finished the story affirming, "That's great Betty Bean." I was feeling very special indeed. Later that night the newscaster shared the presidential couple's arrival in Houston showing a film clip and I could swear I saw myself on TV, waving to the president although no one else did. President Kennedy went on to give a speech at the Rice Hotel that evening, Thursday, November 21, 1963.

It was a regular school day, Friday, November 22, 1963. We had finished our regular class work and Sister Catherine Marie was rewarding us by reading out loud as she often did in the afternoon. Mother Superior, our school principal came and interrupted the class calling Sister Catherine Marie out of the room, which she had never done before. We all immediately knew something was up or someone was in trouble. She left for a few minutes, returning very upset, rattled, visibly shaken, a stricken look on her face as she told us in the calmest voice she seemed to be able to muster that President Kennedy had been shot and was dead. Shot in Dallas his next stop on his Presidential tour of Texas.

I heard no words after that although I know she was speaking. I'm sure she did not know what she was saying either. A slow motion pandaemonium set in. We were all in shock just as the nation was in shock. Some kids fell to their knees on the floor wailing, some just sat and cried openly, tears rolling down their cheeks, others stood in protest, others incredulously asked out loud in disbelief, "What? NO!!" Laying my head on my desk I immediately fell apart, collapsing in tears.

My world changed... the nation changed... the whole world changed that day. School ended early; it was useless to try to teach. No one could function as grief and shock took over. Parents were called and when mother arrived to pick me up at school instead of me running to the car she had to come and find me standing against a brick wall. The nuns had led everyone out side to wait for parents but I was inconsolable, unable to move, in shock. Returning home we turned on the news to hear about the assassination, about how he was shot in the back seat of the very same type car he drove in when we saw them only the day before. We watched in disbelief as they played the film of beautiful Mrs. Kennedy in her elegant suit attempting to help him, covered in her husband's blood. It was too much to bear. I learned the meaning of the word assassination first hand that day, a word that had never been in my vocabulary.

My father returned home early from work. Everything had come to an abrupt halt at NASA as well with the news of President Kennedy's assassination. Clearly visibly shaken, sullen, pale and abnormally quiet I knew he and mom were deeply hurting. I hadn't seen them like that since my sister Patty had died years earlier. He walked in the back door from the garage with a stricken look; instantly mom greeted him with tears and a big hug. They stood together holding on to one another for a very long time, then went to sit and watch the horrible news reports on TV. We sat in the den as a family detached from reality, in disbelief as we listened to the nightmare. Our hero, our president, the bigger than life man I had just seen the day before, the Irish Catholic president we had celebrated, the man my father had worked for and supported all these years was dead, assassinated, struck down by evil beyond comprehension. Our lives forever changed.

It took some time to recover from President Kennedy's death. The whole nation grieved as we watched his burial on TV. Sister Catherine

Marie brought a TV into the classroom, which was a first at our school, but she was like that. I loved her so much. We watched the burial procession together as a class in silence as the horses carried the coffin of President Kennedy down somber, long Washington D.C. streets. Sounds of crying and sniffling were quietly heard throughout the classroom. We gasped as little John F. Kennedy, Jr. stepped out and saluted his father as the coffin passed. We cried and prayed together for Mrs. Kennedy and the children. Sister Catherine Marie was instrumental in helping us deal with our grief and the reality of death and allowed us to ask questions or talk about how we felt.

Slowly day by day school activities returned to relative normalcy, yet nothing would ever be the same. The innocence of an era was gone. The magic of Camelot was gone. We had a new president in the White house. We all wondered where the country would go from here. How do you recoup from such a traumatic loss? And in our family the question was... what would happen to NASA now without President Kennedy at the helm.

Under the Johnson administration NASA thankfully moved forward, honoring President Kennedy's declaration to put a man on the moon in three years. More space flights took place and shortly thereafter the Florida NASA Space Center was renamed the John F. Kennedy Space Center. Then, fulfilling Mrs. Kennedy's wish, Cape Canaveral was renamed Cape Kennedy which stayed until 1973 when the state of Florida reinstated the former 400 hundred year old name, Cape Canaveral. Also in 1973 NASA Space Center was renamed the 'Johnson Space Center' in honor of President Johnson as he had served as Chairman of the National Space Council when he was Vice President under President Kennedy and continued his support of NASA efforts as president. It was always difficult for me to remember this new name and for some reason I have continued to call it the NASA Space Center to this day.

Chapter 9

Six For Six

Dad continued to take trips out to sea for space flights and to the tropical island of Bermuda. The Bermuda tracking station was an integral key in space flight and capsule recovery. He loved Bermuda, the island and the people, but most of all he loved just visiting this tropical island, even if it was business oriented. I had grown accustomed to his many business trips away by this time; never growing weary of our wonderful reunions and the interesting, beautiful and sometimes funny presents he brought home for the family. One time he even brought home chocolate covered ants which we never opened.

A new set of nine more astronauts for the Gemini Project was ceremoniously revealed at a NASA press conference on September 17, 1962. My biggest concern at this point was how would I fit all their pictures on my wall. This new chosen elite created much excitement for the next phase of the journey in moving forward to achieve the goal of putting man on the moon. Simply referred to as Group 2, also known as 'The New Nine' the group included: Neil Armstrong, Frank Borman, Charles 'Pete' Conrad Jr., James Lovell Jr., James McDivitt,

Thomas Stafford, Edward White, John Young, and Elliott See who died in a plane crash before he could complete his slated mission on Gemini 9.

The culmination of the Mercury project was an apex of "Six for Six" with Gordon Cooper's, Faith 7, launch on May 15,1963 the longest, 22 orbital, Mercury flight in history. Gordy, as Dad called him, was the first man to sleep in space. Mercury had become automated over the years. Chuck Yeager, whose bitterness for having been left out of the original seven clearly had still not been assuaged, remarked Mercury astronauts were nothing more than "Spam in a Can." Apparently, the reasoning behind this statement was all Mercury flights by that time were fully automated, virtually controlled by Mission Control. Some surmised that the astronauts weren't really flying at all, which I always found to be ludicrous. Proof of that was every astronaut manually controlled the capsule throughout flights at different times. On more than one occasion had it not been for their brilliant decision making, fast thinking and skillful hands-on maneuvers, disaster would have been inevitable. Mission control's automated control was just added assurance that if anything went wrong they not only had a brilliant and well-trained astronaut to make the final call but also Mission Control to guide them along where necessary. My retort at the time was, "How else is an astronaut alone in space going to get some sleep?"

After his retirement in 1976 "Chuck" Yeager was honored at a special White House ceremony. He was the first person to fly faster than the speed of sound at a time when supersonic flight was considered extremely hazardous, also later he became the first man to fly twice the speed of sound. Not forgetting the dare devil move which made him the unofficial first man in space as he secretly flew his plane up, out and back into the atmosphere, Yeager retired as 'Air Force Brigadier General', Charles "Chuck" Yeager' and given a special silver medal which was equal to a noncombat Medal of Honor by President Ford. A true flying cowboy and very true to his nature he flew one last supersonic flight in a Phantom F-4 in 1975 before retiring. He flew in every war including the Viet Nam war. A monument statue honoring his years of space flight stands at Edwards Air Force Base, California.

Simultaneously as NASA advanced from the single manned flight to twin Gemini spacecraft missions, the British Invasion came to America. A moment forever embedded in my mind on February 9,1964, laying on the green cloverleaf carpet in our den, on my stomach, elbows down, chin propped on hands, eyes riveted on the TV screen, barely able to contain my excitement as the Beatles made their U.S. debut on the Ed Sullivan show. He introduced them as the "Youngsters from Liverpool. Here they are!

The Beatles!" The Fab Four broke into song amid screaming fans, singing, "All My Loving, Till There Was You, She Loves You, Yeah, Yeah, Yeah and I Wanna Hold Your Hand." My heart leapt out of my chest... I was smitten. The hook "I Wanna Hold Your Hand" grabbed the hearts of my friends and I like it was written by Shakespeare and we would not and could not let go. Synchronically, years later I would as I said previously become good friends with Del Shannon who wrote this song for the Fab Four which rocketed them to the top of the charts around the world.

Suddenly the phenomenon of the Beatles was everywhere, a giant part of my life. My new Levis, horseback riding at my friend's ranch and the Beatles was all I needed for nirvana. Dad and mom however were not impressed in the least nor were the nuns at school. They pushed the envelope with their non-conforming, collarless suit jackets, pegged legged pants and bowl-cut, long hair, which was a big departure from the popular flat top, crew cut hair styles of the day. The long mop haircuts and harmonization were not to my dad's liking at all. His harmonization ran toward Barbara Shop Quartets. To my parents they were the antithesis of clean cut. However, dad finally conceded that John Lennon was "pretty good." My parents were even less impressed with the bad boy Rolling Stones and Bob Dylan and agreed then that the Beatles weren't so bad after all.

We were happy. Life was extremely good enjoying friends, family, church, school and all the great sports, activities and parties in our lives. Then shockingly dad and mom called a family meeting. Sitting in our den we heard the dreaded words that would forever change the course of our lives. It was the end of 1964 and as my parents shared the totally unexpected news all the plans for my brother's and my chosen high schools were utterly, disappointedly squashed. There we sat in disbelief listening as Dad shockingly announced that we would again be moving. I was just completing the seventh grade with plans for an all girls Catholic high school. Dennis was ready to move on to his chosen all boys high school along with his friends. Yet there were mom and dad telling us we were leaving Houston, for his new job assisting his boss Walt Williams who was just appointed General Manager of the Aerospace Corporation in California. It was the first time I'd heard the word Aerospace.

Reflecting back to the family meeting in Virginia when we were told about our move to Houston there clearly was no joy in this announcement as there had been then. We were flatly told we would be renting out our wonderful Houston home for a time then, eventually, selling it.

Dad chose instead to move to new horizons loyally following his boss Walt Williams, as he had done for all the previous moves. They were a team, his job at NASA was complete, Mercury was Six for Six and it was time to move on to a new job and a new challenge. The specific task of Mercury was to orbit a manned spacecraft around the Earth, research and study the results on humans as they operated successfully in microgravity, study the effects of space travel on man and recover both the astronauts and the spacecraft safely. This project was complete.

All my effort went into fighting the move to no avail, even seeking out Sister Catherine Marie's help to beseech my parents to work something out to allow me to stay in Houston with friends. I was just a child, self centered, dramatic, very tired of moving and loosing friends, not understanding dad's career. They were patient with me but the decision was made and there were no choices about it. Sullenly and angrily Dennis and I begrudgingly complied. We housed Ginger in a shelter where she would live without me for up to a year as she was not allowed to move with us. We had no home to move to, just like previous moves we would be staying in a hotel. Then both our families performed the ritual we had all come to know too well. We packed up and moved on ...

this time retracing our steps back to California.

Moon Child: Growing Up NASA

Part 4

California
Back To Where We Started

Aerospace

Music was my refuge. I could crawl into the space between the notes and curl my back to loneliness.

~ Maya Angelou, Gather Together in My Name

Chapter 1

Los Angeles

It was 1964; we were living in a beautiful house in Houston one month and the next month all our belongings were stored away for yet another moving van delivery to an undecided destination. I learned later that dad left NASA to work on the technical development of the Titan III Rocket at Aerospace with his boss Walt Williams; however at the time I didn't care what he was working on, mourning the loss of our home and Houston family.

The only information I retained at the time was that dad was leaving NASA for Aerospace somewhere in Los Angeles California. Ginger was housed in a kennel for an indefinite amount of time until we could summon for her. Again, our family of four embarked on the all-American road trip across country. This expedition, the flip-side from our joyous hope filled move to Houston, was a sullen and somber trip for my brother and I.

The trip was joyless and I hold very few memories of it except for the typical Stuckey's and Howard Johnson stops. Dad just wanted to 'get us there.' Mother was the only one who embraced this decision to move to California as she reveled in her returning 'home'. Although the move was really no different from any of our previous abrupt moves with NACA or NASA, my brother and I felt this one deeply. Like happily growing plants ripped from fertile soil, we languished in transplant shock. This move shook us to the quick.

Somehow I always felt as if dad felt great disappointment about this move as well. He did not carry the same enthusiasm for work or life as in previous assignments. Mom exuberantly prearranged for happy reunions with old friends. She was unable to mask her joy, which was at complete odds to the sorrow of losing our friends and home, which inevitably built a wall between us for sometime to come. It took my brother and I many years to adjust to being uprooted, if in fact we ever did. It was a very hard age for both of us to abandon everyone and all our high school plans. In years to come, I deeply felt we had abandoned not only our home but the path of a positive future. It was this move which brought us to a fork in the road which inevitably led us on the lower path of alcoholism and addiction as we became unable to deal with our emotions and pain. The perpetuity of "nomadism" in our lives, culminating with this decision, set into motion an eventual downward spiraling effect in our teenage lives, slowly at first and then with full force. There was no escape from the pain of loss. There simply would never be the security of permanency. However this book is about Moon Child: Growing up NASA not Moon Teen or Adult gone out of control so, therefore, I won't delve into the results of a nomadic life and the pain of a child's lost hope. However I will say many poor decisions in my life resulted from the driving force within me which pushed unsuccessfully to make the painful, bottomless emptiness subside. However, that is possibly all for another book one day.

In California, we were thrust into a drastically harsh and different way of life from the friendly, warm, big spirited embrace of Texas. When first arriving in sunny California, we stayed in a dark and dreary hotel for some time, The Carriage House Inn on Van Nuys Blvd. At the time it boasted a nice restaurant where dad loved to take us out daily to dinner and breakfast. Mom, on the other hand, unceasingly complained about overspending for expensive family meals, pushing for a room with a kitchenette where she could prepare food to feed us on a budget. None were available.

At one such dinner out I dressed up in my nicest gray, wool skirt, frilly white blouse and black flats. Carrying my new, black, leather, bucket purse from Houston, which held my saved allowance nicely tucked inside, I held it on the crook of my arm in a grownup fashion just like mom. We marched as a family from the hotel room to the restaurant, where in lady-like fashion, I placed my new purse under my chair at our table while I partook in a fried oyster three course dinner. After desert, dad left the attentive waiter a tip, we abandoned our table to return to our room. Upon opening the hotel door, I panicked, realizing I'd forgotten my purse at the restaurant. Mom was not happy with my careless, thoughtless actions and scolded me harshly until I was ready to cry. Dad patted me on the head, took me by the hand comforting me, soothing, "Don't worry. It's ok we'll go get it. It's probably right where you left it. Come on. Things like this can happen."

Hand-in-hand, we returned immediately to retrieve it. Dad explained the situation to the manager who conferred off to the side with the dinner staff. He returned stating no such thing was left behind and our waiter had gone home. In disbelief I gave a detailed description to him, let go of my dad's hand, walked to the table, pointing to where I had left my purse. Again, the manager held discussion between the employees, disappeared into the kitchen and reappeared with my purse in hand. Immediately, checking inside, it was clear it had been gone through and all my allowance stolen. I squealed, "My money is gone! Someone stole my money!" Dad took me by the hand and, without confrontation, we took the purse and left happy that at least the purse was found and returned. Clearly this new dog-eat-dog city we were living in was nothing like friendly, cordial Houston. This was a-water-in-your-face grown up lesson in life. Mom was disgusted that anyone could do this to a child, but angry with me for my absentmindedness and vowed we would be moving out of the expensive hotel immediately, swearing off future expensive dinners out.

Within a few days, we took up temporary quarters as visitors in a most confusing world, the home of my parent's friends, the Mahoney's, in Granda Hills, old friends from NACA days. We bunked with them for a couple of weeks, which worked out to be a very long number of days before they left on vacation.

Mom and Mr. Mahoney clashed constantly every night at dinner as she openly voiced her opinion about this or that. He clearly was a bitter man and jealous of my father's success with NASA. Even more, he didn't approve of out spoken women. Unrestrained, he unashamedly, boisterously stated women had their place and that place was to keep their mouth shut and do what they were told. This negative, macho attitude, of course, rubbed my mother like an open, oozing blister leading to rowdy, loud, confrontational 'discussions'.

I'd never seen or experienced this behavior before and was scared speechless. Mrs. Mahoney, use to his out bursts, was embarrassed and fearful. She shyly and demurely chided and shushed her husband, often times taking a verbal attack in the process. Every night of our stay, she would hesitantly, gently send him from the dinner table down the hall with a newspaper in hand to the 'john' telling him to calm down. After a long, quiet time, as we all waited for the other shoe to drop, he'd emerge from the bathroom and take root in his lazy boy chair, where he would sit sullen and angry the rest of the night, thankfully refusing to speak to anyone and finally fall asleep.

Dad would walk mom out to the back patio for long talks in an effort to calm her down, get her to stay quiet and keep the peace. After a while, she would return to help with dishes, biting her lip until the next night's blow out. Mom's tenacious spirit would not allow her to ever back down as she had the heart of a woman's rights activist long before it was fashionable. She completely disapproved of Mr. Mahoney's treatment of his wife and children, becoming protective in a very sisterly way. Ironically Mrs. Mahoney's name was Betty. She was a sweet, demure, kind Catholic lady who walked on egg shells to please everyone in her home. She spent her married life at her husband's and son's beckon call.

Their boys were duplicates of their father, bullying the weaker incessantly, which happened at the time to be their little sister, me and their mother, the worst of it landing on the mother, Betty. Peace gratefully came and we could breathe again when the Mahoney's went on a three week vacation while we house sat for them and searched for our own house to rent. Thankfully, before their return from vacation we found a house and simultaneously moved into it the same day of their return.

The day of their vacation departure the daughter who was younger than myself awarded me the honorable task of caring for her secret white, pet rat which lived in a shoe box in her room so that her father and brothers would not know she had it.

Her mother secretly supplied whatever food was needed. Apprehensively I agreed to care for the cute little pink nosed rodent, which was the one and only time I willingly allowed a rat in my life, as I felt sorry for the sad little girl and the rat. I missed Ginger immensely, so much so that even a furry short haired rat brought joy and a sense of peace. Alone in their home I was now free to play my music without interruption. Having been introduced to the Beach Boys. I'd listen and sing along to California Girls and Little Deuce Coop with visions of blonde, beach surfers in Hawaiian shirts, surf boards and woody, station wagons filling my head. At the same time, I learned rodents can be fun, enjoying the new friend very much, letting the rat crawl up and down my arm and over my shoulders where she would sometimes even fall asleep. Me and the rat became 'we', temporary friends in a transit world. Years later, when Michael Jackson would sing of Ben, my understanding of his rat friendship was immediate and heartfelt.

Chapter 2

Hanna and Etough Streets

Gratefully free of the Mahoney's, we moved into a two story rental in the hilly, north San Fernando Valley suburb of Canoga Park, just about an hour drive for dad to Aerospace in El Segundo. Mom and dad concluded the drive was a typical Los Angeles drive, believing the fallacy that freeways would help speed the commute. Unlike the small town of Lancaster, traffic and distance was just something you lived with in Los Angeles, driving distance always measured in time and traffic congestion... not miles.

The original owners of the rental had just recently moved because of divorce. Being raised Catholic divorce was a taboo subject, an uncommon thing in those days. Only the failed, promiscuous or movie stars experienced divorce but never Catholics. At this time, there had never been anyone in my known protected world who had been divorced. While nosing around through the house, I discovered an abandoned wedding album in the empty hall closet under the stairs. Inquisitive, I pulled it from the highest shelf where it sat purposely shunned, wondering what type of person divorces, with curious apprehension, I carefully opened the white leather cover. Peering down at a bright picture of a glowing, beaming, happy bride and groom gushing back at me, I was struck by the stark contrast to the feeling in the house which matched my own heavy weighted feelings of abandonment and loss. I wondered what could have turned their lives to such sadness forcing them to leave this gorgeous book, nice house and their lives together behind. In that split second I felt the ripping emptiness and loneliness of their lives pervasively encompass me. Sitting on the floor staring at the wedding book spread out before me with trepidation, I softly questioned mom about what she thought could have happened to them, to their lives.

There might well have been a murder in that house as she retaliated with repulsion. She stormed over, snatched up the album, muttering something under her breath I could not quite make out, asked, "Where did you find this?" I pointed to the closet. She snapped the book shut, gripping it tightly and phoned the realtor to ask if they had mistakenly forgotten the album. Clearly the answer was, "No." She marched out the back door to the trash bin, where I watched through the sliding, patio-door as she unceremoniously deposited it in the trash bin. Divorce was not a topic for discussion in a Catholic home. I felt the haunting emptiness of that house in my bones. There was no point in making friends as I'd soon lose them anyway so I retreated within myself to music and records, yearning for a sense of stability and permanency.

At long last, mom announced we'd be sending for Ginger. This was absolute music to my ears and joy to my solitary heart. Barely able to contain myself, counting the days until my friend, companion and confidant would be with me again. Mom and dad arranged to have her flown in on a special pets only flight, finally releasing her from the lonely far away kennel. It had been several long months until we finally found this rental which allowed a dog. Dad joked that the flight for Ginger which cost $1.06 was more expensive than driving the family to California. I chided him, "Dad, don't say that. It's Ginger!"

Our reunion was a joyous, tearful occasion; even mom's eyes welled up with tears. We traveled as a family the night of her flight to Los Angeles International Airport, where we found the baggage and pet cargo hangar. As we entered the hangar, Ginger's yelping in a distant cage was recognizable as she heard our voices. Hopping from foot to foot I was unable to stand still calling out to her, "Ginger! It's okay we're here girl! Ginger! I'm here!" The stewards took our name, unceremoniously pulled her cage out from the back, opened the door and she gleefully wiggled uncontrollably out of the cage, ears back, wagging her body with her still crooked tail. Joyously she leapt into my arms licking my face. I was finally reunited with my sweet friend, smothering her in kisses and hugs. Our drive home that night was euphoric, our family complete again. Mom was so happy to see Ginger, delighted with my joy, so much so that she didn't even scream too loud upon our arrival home when Ginger, who had been caged for hours during her long flight, wee-wee'd a river all over the rental's beautiful, dining room, parquet floor. However, nothing she did could upset us. Yes, we were finally reunited, my faithful friend and I together again.

Music was still a grounding point for me as Motown and the Supremes connected me to my 'home' in Houston. The Beach Boys were catchy, but the Beatles became my constant companions. I met my first California friends at school as we bonded over the movie "A Hard Days Night." We were struggling to resettle and the space program, sadly, now seemed distant; however, dad kept us updated with incidental reports, always keeping tabs, watching every launch on TV.

Project Gemini was moving forward quickly throughout 1965. Although dad worked in El Segundo at Aerospace, he continued regular business trips to Houston, still keeping in touch with all his friends. Gus Grissom soared back into space with John Young in Gemini III, which made three orbits around the earth and was nick named 'Molly Brown' for the popular Broadway play at the time the 'Unsinkable Molly Brown' which elicited howling laughter from dad. It was an amazing feat to have two astronauts together in space. Each new flight marked a significant place in history. We watched James McDivitt and Ed White's flight and held our breath in absolute awe as Ed White became the first man to 'walk in space,' as he floated weightless in space tethered to the space capsule. It was a nail biter which prompted many questions for dad about his safety and we were assured all precautions were taken.

The familiar voice of Deke Slayton, 'the old man' as dad referred to him, stayed in constant communication from Mission Control while he viewed the earth and universe as the first American to float in space. Deke, one of the original astronauts, had become the voice of Mission Control in 1962, serving over the years as Director of Flight Crew Operations after being grounded from flight when the doctors found a heart murmur. Later, of course, that would not hinder him as he became honored to be the oldest man in space on the very last Apollo flight. He flew as the docking module pilot in the Apollo-Soyuz Test Project which was the first joint U.S. and Soviet space flight.

Then dad's good friend Gordon Cooper and Pete Conrad spent an entire week in space in Gemini V. Pushing the envelope further, Gemini VII, manned by Frank Borman and dad's good friend James Lovell, proved that man could live in space for two weeks at a time. Also marking this time in history, Gemini VI-A manned by Wally Schirra and Tom Stafford, joined Gemini VII in space and completed this historic mission with the first successful space rendezvous.

Years later as I sorted through mom's extensive piles of saved letters and cards, I found the 1965 Christmas card to my parents from James Lovell and his wife commemorating this historic flight. Also on this rendezvous, Wally Schirra, my childhood crush, entertained the world on the last of the December 1965 Gemini flights, in holiday fashion with his rendition of Jingle Bells, which he played on his smuggled onboard harmonica. I still remember dad's warm chuckle as he stood before the TV where we watched together in the den, listening to his friend play this holiday song and wish the world a Merry Christmas. Dad spoke to the TV as if I wasn't present, "Schirra, how'd you smuggle that onboard? Good for you." Then shaking his head and laughing saying, "This ought to be a good story."

In 1965 the British invasion also pumped out 'The Dave Clark Five' and 'Herman's Hermits'. I loved to hop around singing 'Mrs. Brown You've Got a Lovely Daughter' replicating Peter Noone's jumping jack type dance. Dad rather liked the jib of that song too. We'd sing it together only he'd change the lyrics to 'Mrs. Byrnes You've Got a Lovely Daughter' then we'd do his favorite dance, the polka. On a Saturday afternoon, Herman's Hermits would be singing from the screen on the Shindig show and before you knew it, surrounded by the smell of barbecued chicken from the turning rotisserie spit dad tended on the patio, we'd be dancing the polka around the den, our feet moving in unison over the familiar cloverleaf rug, a fond repeat of little girl dances with daddy in Lancaster.

Ginger would bark and join in the fun running along next to us. My heart was happy again in those fleeting moments.

One constant in all our homes for years, until the house in Canoga Park where it was rolled up and stored in the garage, not to be used again until I moved out and took it with me, was that familiar large, green, cloverleaf, throw rug. This extra large, wool, roll out rug graced the floor in all our homes in California, Virginia and Texas and now back to California again. In 1965, our furniture and trappings, such as this rug, brought a sense of continuity and consistency in a life of transitory "nomadism" from rental to rental. Unintentionally, like a life preserver at sea, I grasped onto these material possessions. The thick slab, walnut, coffee table and side tables with the 50s, black, wrought iron 'V' legs dad proudly made for our family in Lancaster, wood shop class and the flying geese he creatively hung just so in an ascending flight pattern on wall after wall of every den in every house we ever lived in and like a comfortable old friend, the cloverleaf rug. It was on the wool, cloverleaves I'd lay, nose glued to the TV whether it was a black and white box console or a newer portable on wheels. Somehow it grounded me. In Lancaster watching The Mickey Mouse Club, in Virginia watching Del Shannon on American Bandstand, in Texas watching the Beatles on the Ed Sullivan Show, then again in California watching the Dave Clarke Five on Shindig I was always on that rug. I watched every space launch and landing on that rug. Many moments in history were viewed on TV on that rug while mom either sat on the divan watching too or lovingly puttered in the kitchen, conjuring up home cooked meals for her family. The familiar, comforting aroma of mom's pressure cooker beef stew or ham bone soup, hot dog and bean or tuna casseroles wafted soothing aromas through the house, filling the senses as I laid tummy down feet up, chin on hands on that cloverleaf rug.

With the church, school and rental area decided we were, as always, faithfully enrolled into the local Catholic school, this time at Our Lady of the Valley. The church and school again were our family compass and grounding point. No matter what rental we lived in, we continued to attend the same Catholic school and church. My brother, however, now was older and in high school, or what would be Jr. High School today. He was enrolled in the only all boys Catholic high school at our end of the San Fernando Valley, Chaminade. He was given no choices in California. Understandably, it was determined not feasible for mom, who hated driving in this big city, to drive miles to take him daily to a school on the other side of the valley. He found very quickly this school didn't measure up to the boy's high school he had chosen in Texas. Soon his unhappiness and the feeling of not fitting in erupted. He acted out, getting into fist fights resulting in expulsion, then was re-enrolled in a public school, Chatsworth High School. My parents were beside themselves as public school was a first for us and felt like failure. However, their anxiety was assuaged as Dennis soon seemed to happily adjust socially, academically and enthusiastically joined the Chatsworth football team. Also, they were very happy to learn there were other children in the public high school who attended our Catholic church, one of them from the football team, Brian Rochelle, who became Dennis' best friend. For me, it was all very exciting to know Dennis was breaking the rules and doing the unheard of, attending a public school.

In California elementary school, Dad's movies from Aerospace were not as captivating as the NASA movies in Houston and seemed to only give us time off from daily school work. There was not the interest or enthusiasm for them as in Texas. As a result, movie days only happened once or twice... then ceased.

I struggled to fit in as well, unable to muster any joy. I felt disconnected from my wonderful friends in Texas. There was no sense of school football spirit in the California Catholic schools... or any football for that matter. The girls volleyball team only played at recess and basketball was the only after school sport for the boys. There was no school spirit, no push to win or turn out for games. There was no school basketball court or gym so the team was forced to practice and hold games at the local neighborhood park. The nuns frowned on cheer squads and, apparently, felt girls jumping in short skirts, yelling cheers with pompoms was a bit too grown up for the elementary school children. They tried to direct and encourage me to play the game of volley ball. I had experienced the sport of volley ball in Texas, enduring several sprained fingers. As a result, it was the one sport I loathed and I refused to take part. Instead much to the nun's chagrin, I persisted in attempting to rally the girls at recess and after school hours for an unsanctioned basketball cheer squad. Although most resisted for fear of the nuns disapproval, I was able to recruit three other girls, my Beatles buddies. We designed cheer squad uniforms with tie dyed shoe laces and royal blue pleated skirts, constructed homemade pompoms from blue and white crepe paper and conducted cheer practice in my front yard several days a week after school. When the basketball games began we cheered at several games, however, disappointingly, the girls and the team did not have the enthusiasm for winning or cheering I had experienced with Texas football. Soon, much to the nuns and my parents relief, I lost interest.

Surrendering to California ways, I abandoned all hope for cheer, turning back to music, the Beatles, my records, the latest dances on American Bandstand and a whole new level of interest in boys. Still feeling lost, not fitting in the attraction to the 'bad' kids in school drew me in. An exciting, secret, conniving interest in ditching school set in.

Transitioning to another rental two streets over, we enjoyed the California pleasure of a swimming pool year round. The choice of this rental felt like mom had given us a year round Christmas present until she warned, "Enjoy it now because it will be the last pool we ever have." She held true to her word as the upkeep was not in her budget. However, this temporary home was brighter, lighter and had a much better hopeful feel to it. Dennis took up the guitar and began a garage band. Much to my enjoyment, albeit my brothers everlasting wish for me to stop dogging him, he allowed me only occasionally to sit in on band practices which were immensely interesting for me, as well as the boys in the band as I became their groupie. I can still hear the rendition of definitely their best song the Animals', House of the Rising Son.

Dad's astronaut friends continued to make space history with the fast moving Project Gemini throughout 1966, reaching record heights and orbits, achieving unfathomable feats. At the same time America's answer to the British, 'The Monkees' TV show crashed on the scene in 1966 along with Nancy Sinatra's 'These Boots Are Made For Walking.' White "pleather" boots and mini skirts, which were a 'must have', were given the prime spotlight in every California girls wardrobe. I remember proudly strutting a mini skirt and boots down the drive way to get into dad's new blue Chevy Impala. He was stretching his limits moving away from a plain white car. Mom's car on the other hand was a jaunty, white Mustang with red interior, considered an economy car at the time. Teen magazines about Twiggy taught me how to apply black and white eye liner to create giant, contrasting eyelashes, which shocked both mom and dad the first time I walked out with my painted on Twiggy look. Summer Blonde was applied weekly to achieve the California sun drenched highlights required to accompany heavy, black, winged eyeliner and turquoise eye shadow. Flat ironed hair took the place of brush rollers and dryer caps. At first, mom was thrilled to see me take an interest in her iron and ironing board until she realized I was only ironing my hair and not the pile of clothes in the laundry room.

TV Movies became a source of wonderful solitary entertainment and escape as I rolled the portable black and white TV into my room, adjusted the bunny ear antenna just so for the best reception and watched Fred Astaire and Gene Kelly dance, Bob Hope and Bing Crosby in their road movies and Danny Kaye, to name just a few. I loved to watch the movement of the dancers glide across the screen. The 'Rat Pack' was at its peak and my admiration for Sammy Davis Jr. hit an all time high as I watched all possible performances and read his autobiography more than once. Dad's favorite from the Rat Pack was Dean Martin, I had to agree he was very handsome and charismatic with a smooth, melodic singing voice. He was so suave, his singing so effortless. Dusty Springfield was singing 'Wishing and Hoping'. I was singing along with Dusty in the car one day when Dad quizzically asked, "Why do you like that song so much, Betty?"

Immediately I blurted out in a pleading voice, "Because I wish and hope we can move back to Houston someday."

Dad continued contact with his friends at NASA traveling there for business often. I was so jealous, longing and begging to travel 'home' with him. Following my mother's footsteps in the art of letter writing, we kept free flowing, faithful, constant contact with friends by letter. Long distance calls were a rare and special event for contact with close family members in emergencies only. Dad appeased my begging by relaying messages for me when he attended Sunday Mass at St. Christopher's while on his trips.

Time marched on slowly. Over two years after moving back to California our melancholy still had not lifted, not even trips to the Topanga Plaza mall record store or the Kern River could assuage it. Mom and dad had renewed the inexpensive, fun family vacation tradition of trips to the Kern River, the Sierra Mountain vacation spot we enjoyed in the early '50s as a young family along with pilots and other NACA families. Having grown now, it was safe for us children to rough it in camping trailers at Headquarters Campground every summer. We would camp in the trailer and enjoy climbing rocks and swimming in the slow pools of the fast moving river by day and star gazing and bonfires by the river at night. Dad and Dennis loved to fish, providing a bonding experience which evolved throughout the years. Later in life, I would continue this Kern River vacation tradition, packing up my own children for fun excursions to the river, camping out under the stars. Memories of Scott Crossfield's fly over as dad held me in his arms would spring to mind as jets from Edwards – out on night time test flights – roared down over the river and thru the canyon. Many times in the inky darkness, pilots nodding and waving at us from lit cockpits gave my family and river side campers a magnificent thrill.

We had been in California by this time for almost three years when mom and dad called another dreaded family meeting. Dennis and I begrudgingly drug into the living room, expecting to hear the same old drill that we were moving again. These type family meetings were always the announcement of a move to a different state. Moves to new rentals never required a family meeting. However, this time we were surprisingly astounded with the news. They explained they understood how we both missed Houston and our friends. We sat dumbfounded at first, not believing our ears as they explained they were flying us as a family to Texas for a month long summer vacation while they sold our Houston house. The joy of returning 'home' countered and outweighed the unabashed sadness and disappointment over the finality of selling our beautiful home, which signaled we definitely were never moving back. Nevertheless our hearts soared, spirits lifted with news of reunions on the horizon. Immediately we bounded off with squeals of joy to pack our suitcases. Within the week we were onboard a Continental 747 jet, two by two, with mom and dad seated directly in front of me and Dennis.

On our flight to Houston International Airport we traveled in style. Dennis allowed me the window seat on the flight there, while a smiling, stewardess in a tailored skirt uniform, silk nylons and high heels, her hat perfectly placed and tilted just so, gracefully served peanuts, Shirley Temple and Davy Crockett drinks along with cocktails for mom and dad on our downward trays. Within a short time, the wheels touched down and rolled to a stop near our old home at the very familiar airport where I used to ride my bike to catch a glimpse of movie stars, only this time we were the ones disembarking. Breathing in deeply, I filled my senses with the familiar sustaining smell of Houston air, I was 'home'. Simply ecstatic! That wonderful friendly Texas spirit greeted us. Both my brother and I were welcomed and embraced, staying overnight with friends for days on end in familiar, friendly homes. Many parties were held in mom and dad's honor. We stayed in a large hotel where we gathered in the game room to play pool while parents dined in the hotel restaurant bar with friends. Here spontaneous parties would materialize creating much fun. We danced, laughed, loudly played our music singing to "Unchained Melody" by the Righteous Brothers, the Temptations' "My Girl" and of course many Beatles songs.

Disproving the axiom, 'You can never go home again,' our lives for those brief few weeks returned to Houston normalcy. Reconnecting with an old crush, Tommy Sudela, my biggest dream came true as I finally saw him look at me as I had always dreamed he would. This time there was no singing, "It's My Party And I'll Cry If I Want To" as he became my first sweet summer love. The entire visit was a huge 'love fest' party. I begged my parents to allow me to continue to live there with friends and attend my chosen high school. Although my pleas were ardently denied, it was a joyful, ecstatic trip back 'home'. I felt grateful to my parents for making it possible, a dream come true, affording us memories for a lifetime.

For decades I called Houston, Texas my 'real' home. We all vowed to continue to communicate, letters were steady at first, then slowed as my friends in Houston moved on to Catholic high school and other interests we no longer had in common. My attention turned to boys, surfing, sunbathing, bikinis and the beach. Eventually letters ceased altogether, making the transition to California complete; albeit the longing for 'home' and Houston took decades to leave my soul. It would be many, many years before I would become aware I was actually happy living in California, or considered it home. Both Project Gemini and Apollo forged on without the Byrnes family.

Chapter 3

Moorcroft Street

Soon I found myself by default enrolled in an all girl Catholic high school, Louisville High School in Woodland Hills. Just as my brother had experienced the only Catholic girls high school at our end of the valley. There were no co-ed Catholic high schools available. The same disappointment my brother had experienced engulfed me, although drama class was right up my alley and my seamstress skills were a big draw. We wore the typical Catholic school uniforms I had worn in every school I'd ever attended; however designing my own regular clothes was a hit with the girls at school even sewing and selling one design to Cher's neighbor who attended the school.

One creation that won raves of approval was the wide-wale, corduroy, Sonny and Cher type peacoat and matching low rise, mini-skirt with the wide hip belt. Although my home sewn clothes were a hit, the wealthy girls at school found it an oddity that I sewed my own clothes. It seemed no matter what I did I still found myself on the outside, not ever really fitting in. As a result, I pushed the limits to join my brother in public school, rebellious, acting out causing much chaos, ditching classes, smoking in the bathroom. Stealing from purses left unattended in classrooms during assemblies resulted in the first whipping my dad ever administered to me. Dad came into my room with folded belt in hand... still the typical form of chastisement and punishment in those days. This time, crocodile tears didn't discourage nor prevent the whipping. In fact this time, my stubborn teenage arrogance didn't beg not to be hit at all, but instead, incorrigible I rebelliously taunted dad, "Go ahead and hit me! I don't care! I hate my school! I hate my life! I hate you!" Standing defiantly in front of him in my Bermuda short outfit the first stinging, swift licks of the belt hit my bare skin at the thigh and I crumbled to the floor next to my bed, screamed in pain, then clamped my mouth shut. I wouldn't give him the satisfaction of crying out again. Ten times, over and over, I bit my hand hard, leaning on and holding tight to the bed frame for support with each relentless blow. When he finished the whipping I defiantly turned, spitting tearful words in his face, "Do you feel better now? Did that make you feel better to hit me? I still hate you!"

Exasperated and broken, I'll never forget the pain on his face and the defeated look in his eyes as he had no answer for me. He never hit me again. I wish I could say that form of punishment was never used on my brother again but it continued. That was how my parents were raised and unlike today that was how it was done... accomplishing nothing.

Finally and thankfully, my ploy for negative attention paid off, the nuns kindly but firmly asked that my parents move me in lieu of expulsion. Triumphantly I embraced enrollment at Chatsworth High School with my brother and my first true love and boyfriend, Brian Rochelle, also my brother's best friend. Brian and I had become very close and I longed to attend school every day with him. He was simply stunningly handsome, a Roger Moore, James Bond look alike. Even mom embraced Brian as he was genuine, charming, polite and always helpful around the house. He took to our family, fitting right in. I was completely infatuated and the envy of all the girls in school as a new freshman going steady with an older boy. We were told we made a gorgeous couple. Every time I looked at Brian and saw him looking lovingly back, I had to agree. Public school became a new wonderful free-spirited chapter in my life with little focus on academic achievement. Home Ec sewing class was more down my alley as I was thrilled with the freedom to sport my self-made wardrobe to school daily as well.

Not only was it a culture shock in California, but the cost of living was a big bump to mom's frugal budget. It took years to find a more permanent place. Finally with the sale of our Houston house, my parents bought and settled into a San Fernando Valley, ranch style, hilltop, view home on Moorcroft Avenue in Canoga Park. Dad attempted to fulfill the long held wish I'd voiced as a little girl by painting the double front doors bright red in an effort to give me the red house I said I'd always wanted to live in. It was a lovely gesture which touched my heart and looked wonderful.

At night from the backyard, the lights of the city shimmered and glistened like diamonds on black velvet. Here, only chain link fences enclosed the yards to maximize the spectacular view overlooking the San Fernando Valley. As far as the eye could see, all the way to the Santa Monica Mountains, were sporadic twinkling lights which disappeared into black mountain silhouettes propped up in the distance against the contrasting golden moon lit sky. Every night throughout most of the year, you could find my parents stretched out in the overstuffed cushions of the patio lounge chairs drinking their ritual cocktails, enjoying the view of amazing sunsets over the city below. In the winter cold, they were forced inside behind heavily layered decorative, sashed drapes which came with the house. I loved these drapes, but mom thought they were way too fussy preferring simpler furnishings. Here they would sit each night and enjoy the blazing living room, two-way, old stone fireplace. Ginger found much comfort next to dad and mom whether inside or out as they sipped their bourbon and water over ice, reaching down and lovingly petting her as they discussed the day's events, their regular ritual before mom's nightly walk with Ginger up and down the steep neighborhood hills. Sometimes I'd walk with her or take her myself. Ginger never needed a leash although we took one. She was always obedient to come when called, staying close by in her sniffing adventures, yet was never taught to heel.

My room boasted a walk in makeup room and closet area with a large wall size vanity and mirror surrounded by Hollywood type makeup lights. I took full advantage of this vanity, spending many hours mastering makeup techniques and hair styles of the '60s which eventually led to enrolling in beauty college after high school.

Dad and mom were relatively happy to be back in California, especially when visiting old friends... and there were many. Dad still loved to indulge taking his family out for nice dinners in upscale restaurants, a habit I became accustomed to and loved. He started a wonderful tradition, escorting me on late afternoon dinners to restaurants in the valley or at the beach. It was always a special time which called for dressing up. We shared private one-on-one father daughter time during the drive there enjoying a delicious meal and dessert. We'd catch up and generally chat about our lives, my friends and incidental information about his work at Aerospace. In these private times with dad, it seemed to me that I was not the only one missing the Houston way of life. On one such dinner out, he shared about the new logo for NASA. He was surprised to hear I was not a fan of the new logo. I liked the old one with the earth. He laughed at my candor. Time would prove the new NASA logo was for the Space Shuttle, however today the first NASA logo graces all space capsules and space shuttles.

Later I was to learn that his stint with Aerospace was not a happy transition for dad. Following his boss, as he had followed him on all his assignments, did not pan out as he had hoped. He found himself on the outside in Aerospace and the projects he worked on seemed menial and unfulfilling in comparison to those he had enjoyed at NASA for the space race.

The family invested in a new state of the art, walnut wood, stereo console, record player with an AM/FM radio. Set up centrally in the dining room/living room area, music filled the house with a labyrinth of melodic sounds. The new stereo cabinet allowed me to lay claim to the family portable stereo record player. Of course, what made it a stereo was because the speakers could be turned or removed and placed away from the record player as far as the cords would reach. It felt like luxury to have the stereo record player in my bedroom, where I freely played my 33 LPs and 45s. Dad loved to listen to Nat King Cole, Herb Alpert and the Tijuana Brass along with many other big band LPs like Mitch Miller. Mom enjoyed the movie score LPs like Oklahoma or South Pacific which I also loved. Her very favorite was Eddy Arnold's "Make The World Go Away." Music of all sorts reached my soul and gave me a place to express the feelings I had bottled up. Dad also thought Bill Cosby's LPs were hilarious, as did all of us. Saturday afternoons the house would fill with the aroma of barbecue on the spit in the backyard while music filled the house. I, on the other hand, at the far end of the house played the Beatles, Mama's and Papa's, Jose Feliciano and Johnny Mathis, whose smooth velvet voice touched my heart. Also I had great affinity toward the harder edge Jimi Hendrix, The Byrds, Creme, Janis Joplin and of course the amazing Door's, "Come On Baby Light My Fire" rocked my room making the windows vibrate.

Unbeknownst to mom and dad, I happily adjusted into my teen years with the aid of marijuana and other drugs as the 'Love Child' hippie faze of the late '60s took root in my life. My brother, too, immersed himself in the hippie culture of drugs, love and rock n' roll. He was a constant 'groovy' source of supply for me. Brian, protected me from harder drugs to some extent. My clothes design and sewing hit its peak in high school as many of my friends put in requests for my hippie style, paisley, sleeveless jumpsuits... my first entrepreneurial skill put to use to earn money for my weed. Each hippie jumper was, of course, adorned with self strung long bead and seed necklaces.

Dad's rolling laugh was still a warm blanket for me when he was not gone on business trips to Houston and was home relaxing. We spent many happy hours sitting in the hall den watching our new color Zenith TV console, giggling along with the "Laugh In" crowd until we cried. Mom preferred reading her magazines and newspapers in the kitchen den. She became bored as we grew, leaving her with less to care for at home, so she went back to a nursing job working the swing shift at the Motion Picture Retirement Home, which lasted for a year or so before she permanently retired. Always with a need to give, she volunteered and worked throughout the rest of her life in the Catholic church St. Vincent de Paul Society thrift stores.

My life became engulfed with boys and the beach, before long I was a complete Flower Child Hippie, with all the drinking and drugs that came with the era. The years became blurry and a downward spiral at times but that is all for another book about survival and God's saving grace. Suffice it to say several of my friends did not survive those years. There were many funerals, including Brian's, which completely devastated me. His death due to drugs sent me cascading out of control. If it had not been for my father and his secure, strong, stalwart love as he literally stood by me, driving me to the cemetery to sit at Brian's grave site while I cried a river of tears as I said goodbye, I would not have survived either. Brian was the first true love of my life. I will always love and miss him. Dad knew that and never once judged me or criticized me nor made any attempt to encourage me not to feel the pain. He just stood by me with centered, rooted allegiance, silently loving me, which he continued to do throughout my teens, in and out of many horrific situations which would have been disheartening for any parent. After Brian, I settled for less favorable, abusive and destructive relationships. No matter what situation I got myself into, mom and dad were always there, the one sure thing I could always turn to in life.

Although we were not involved directly as a family with NASA in Houston any longer in the mid '60s, no matter what was happening in our crazy lives, time stood still for every space event. NASA and space flight were still the hub, the grounding point of our lives, pulling us together from other interests and bonding us forever. I will always cherish the times I sat in front of the TV with my mom or dad watching space flights.

The day Apollo 11 landed on the moon, I sat with dad in our little hall den in California as we nervously stood, then sat, then stood, then paced around the room, finally freezing, eyes locked on the TV screen as Neil Armstrong took his first steps onto the moon. I didn't realize until many years later how truly blessed I was to be alone with dad on that very special day. Although I know he longed to be at the Cape with the crew, as he had been for so many launches and space flights for years, for me, the look on my father's face of utter complete rapture, the sense of true accomplishment for many long years of hard work is something I will never forget. He was speechless for the longest time. We both were. Then with Neil Armstrong's first safe steps down the ladder from Apollo 11, we listened, the world listened, the universe listened as he spoke those words, "One small step for man. One giant leap for mankind", before hopping down to mark the moon's surface with man's first footprints. Dad could not contain his joy shaking his head up and down in agreement, and pumping his fist in the air, "Yes! By God! That's it! Yes! Very good!" We just kept watching and listening to Mission Control and the astronauts talk back and forth while the astronauts walked on the moon. Dad blurted out over and over, "That's It! Yes! By God! That's It! By God we've done it!" A day and feeling I will never forget.

Dad was home this day not by coincidence but because he planned it that way. His life had slowed down considerably. He needed to be home. He'd had heart surgery by this time as he suffered from a heart condition caused by Scarlet Fever as a boy, aggravated and advanced due to hard, stressful living, heavy drinking and smoking which came with the era of the '60s.

He had gone in for tests on his heart and suffered a major heart attack on the doctor's exam table. His heart surgery, a new (no pun intended) cutting edge procedure. He had been one of the first in the country to undergo open heart surgery implanting a plastic aortic valve. At the time, there were only two open heart surgeons who had mastered the technique. One ironically and thankfully happened to be located in Houston. His doctor flew him directly to Houston where they sawed open his chest cavity and inserted a nylon aortic valve pump into his failing heart. The heart surgery was performed by the best in the world at the time, Dr. Benton Cooley. The recovery time then was very long. So my parents stayed for over a month and a half in Houston surrounded by friends who loved and supported them.

Dad never once complained or talked about how much pain he was in. However, after returning home he did complain in a joking way about the 'damn' valve keeping him up at night like a ticking clock. We would laugh as we would be sitting in the den watching TV during Laugh In or Bonanza and a quiet moment would come on and all we heard was dad's heart valve pumping ... tick ... tick ... tick. We'd turn and look at him and smile. He'd give a disheartened chuckle and say, "Damn valve!" To me, it was reassuring but for him it was irritating and annoying so he would drink to calm and numb himself so he could fall asleep which was clearly not good for his health. It may sound ghastly; however being the collector that I am I kept some of the stitches from dad's heart surgery, as a reminder to me of his indomitable spirit to live.

Betty Byrnes

Part 5

California

Retirement NASA

"For once you have tasted flight you will walk the earth with your eyes turned skywards, for there you have been and there you will long to return."

~ Leonardo da Vinci

Betty Byrnes

Chapter 1

Back In The Game

After open heart surgery, dad returned to work at Aerospace. His spirit noticeably dampened, he was not happy. He later stated his job there was 'dull' so he made the decision to retire. He moved back into civil service, semi-retired with NASA, where he connected with those making great advances in space flight. Here he felt useful, wanted and needed again near Edwards Air Force Base at NASA Dryden Research Center in the Antelope Valley. Ironically back where he had begun his journey so many years ago with NACA and the X planes. He had a new spring in his step; he was back in the race.... the space race, or as he used to put it, "the airplane business." He was excited to face each new day, working on and juggling twenty different projects at a time... feeling young again. He was always good at wearing many hats and bored unless he was very active.

Project Gemini flights concluded giving way to three man Apollo space flights. Amazing historic flights had taken place as dad whiled away his time at Aerospace and he had felt he was missing out. Now he was a part of something even bigger, the Space Shuttle Program which had begun originally back in the days of the X-15. He was honored to work on and attended the Enterprise roll out, witnessing the historic take off of the Enterprise for Cape Canaveral and its first launch into space.

Ultimately his semi-retirement in 1975 enabled dad to move mom very happily back to where they had begun, back to her favorite place of all time, Lancaster, California. Joining life-long friends who still lived in the Antelope Valley they bought another lovely ranch style, high desert home along with a motor home and traveled the country and into Canada together with Ginger.

In honor of dad's retirement, a huge party was planned by those he worked with from over the years. His friends flew in from Virginia and Texas. I felt so honored that dad invited me and insisted on my attendance. There were a couple hundred people there. Appropriately, as no detail was over looked, the room was set up in a large star shaped seating formation with the orchestra and dance floor at the hub. They quietly played music, guests clinked glasses in toast to dad as we all ate a delicious steak and sea food or chicken dinner. Dad was honored by many speeches, much laughter as well as incredible renderings done by the staff NASA illustrators. An amazing framed picture was put together tying in all his years of work for the space program from the X-1 planes to the Shuttle.

I was so happy for him and it was a huge eye opener for me. He was just my dad and I never saw him in this light. I had always loved dad but to see the open display of appreciation and love for him from this multitude of friends, many of whom I recognized, was simply an astoundingly proud moment for me. He was so proud to have me there as well, introducing me to everyone. I was absolutely thrilled and my heart skipped many beats as I sat across from dad's old friend, Wally Schirra, who graced the head table with us. He was still just as handsome as ever and I still had the same crush on him at 25 as I did when I was a little girl.

Of course although dad was semi retired and working as a consultant for the NASA Space Shuttle program at Dryden, he also continued to reach out into the community to make a difference. He had been a part of United Way while in Houston at NASA and then again a large part of United Way in California, sponsoring and working fund raisers to raise money for the needy throughout his time at Aerospace, which segued after his retirement to an appointment as Antelope Valley District Director of United Way. He also remained a member of the Elks Lodge and continued his involvement with the Knights of Columbus Council. He thoroughly enjoyed gardening and created a backyard farm engineering an amazing compost system, which enabled him to naturally grow vegetables of many varieties.

Nothing he ever did was not researched, studied, intelligently thought out and accomplished. He was a voracious reader and his library contained a vast diversified collection of books; however the bulk were on science, history and space.

Mom and dad also enjoyed traveling, visiting mom's WAC friends along the way, their many friends still in Houston and also family back east in Virginia and New York. Ginger faithfully went along in the motor home on each trip with them until she could no longer make it up the stairs of the camper. Then, it was Dad who took her to the vet to have her put to sleep, saving mom the heartbreak and telling me only after the fact to save me the heartache as well.

In honor of his participation and hard work in the Space Shuttle program, NASA awarded dad with an official industrial model of the Enterprise and Shuttle patch, just as he had received for previous space projects. Both mom and dad celebrated and were very much honored to attend two of the Enterprise Space Shuttle landings at Edwards Air Force Base in the Mojave desert as VIP guests in 1976 and 1977. I will never forget the joy and elation on dad's face as he showed me pictures of himself, his bright blue eyes twinkling as he stood in front of the Shuttle at the landing of the Enterprise.

Chapter 2

Things Change Quickly

Shockingly, dad's retirement was quickly cut short by a devastating massive stroke in 1978. He worked through many hours of physical therapy and seemed to be making progress until the day I will never forget.

Deeply asleep that morning a pressing nightmare woke me, a feeling of unbelievable pressure was pushing down on me. In the dream, I was unable to move, barely able to breath, like being pushed underwater and held down by a heavy weight. I had to push with all my might to force myself awake. Still engulfed by a feeling of unrelenting pressure as I woke, I felt there was something terribly wrong with mom and dad. I called the house and there was no answer. I called again; finally mom answered. She was panicked and had called an ambulance. She had been at morning 7:00a.m. Mass, as was her daily routine for decades. Dad had gotten up to dress and had succumbed to another major stroke. He was alone in the house on the floor unable to move until mom returned to help him. He had been calling for me. He battled a long recovery and then in late 1980 lung cancer hit a final blow. Surgery was performed to remove polyps from his lungs and chemotherapy administered twice to no avail. Dad refused further treatment. I will forever be grateful to God that He enabled dad to have those few short years happily at work for NASA again.

Dad still enjoyed sitting out on the patio sipping his bourbon and water over ice even in his illness. So for his birthday one year, I crocheted him a lap blanket and bought him a wooden porch rocking chair which I delivered with much ado in a big, surprise reveal, attempting in my own way to bring some measure of happiness and excitement into his life. His response was not expected. In my entire life I had never heard dad speak out in an opinionated derogatory way toward me but the rocking chair gift elicited a stream of cursing, snarling complaints. I was beside myself and felt horrible that somehow I had hurt him imploring him, "Dad I don't understand. I thought you'd love the rocking chair to sit in on the patio. To relax in while you watch the sunset." I conveyed how sorry I was to upset him and I thought the rocking chair would be easier for him to maneuver in and out of than the low lying lounge chair. My rationalization proving to be a learning experience, a hands on lesson of the old adage 'if it works don't fix it'. Dad adamantly protested saying, "Get that goddamn thing out of here! I'll be damned if I'll sit in that damned thing! I'm not that bad!" I moved it out of the way, walked him back inside with the aid of his walker, out of sight of the rocker, calmed him down finally pulling from him the reason for his reaction.

He explained that my grandmother, who I never knew, had lived a very long, painful life suffering from arthritis of the spine and was confined to a wooden rocking chair or her bed for many years before her death. He had vowed he'd never sit in a rocking chair and wither away like she was forced to do. Understanding, I apologized and quickly volunteered to take the chair home. Then suddenly he softened, acquiesced patting my hand telling me he wanted to sit in the chair for me because I gave him the gift with love. I told him that was not necessary, but he insisted. He did sit in the chair and put the lap blanket on that day, a cold brisk day in winter; however the chair sat on the porch unused every day after that. He would not, however, allow me to remove it. For him it was a gift and symbol of love even if it evoked painful memories and I know it did. In the end it served as a symbol to fight against the flow of illness plaguing his body. The doctors gave dad four months to live, but he defied their odds fighting to live over a full year. Mom stepped up as dad's home nurse, displaying the tenacity and grit which had made her the strong Army nurse she was her entire life. She was never more valiant as when she cared for the love of her life in his last years. Ever the provider, dad moved mom into a fully paid for mobile home where he knew she would be taken care of with very few bills and his steady pension the remainder of her life.

Mom had a hospital bed delivered to the house and moved dad into the front room near the kitchen where he could more easily see out the window to the desert. Weekly regular visits to mom and dad's were the norm and I was blessed to spend many long hours sitting next to dad in this room talking, sharing memories and stories, keeping up to date, sometimes just in silence, sharing moments we both knew we would not have much longer. He gave me his blessing which meant the world to me. I needed to hear he approved of my life, especially after making so many bad choices. I needed to hear that he loved me even though I knew he always had. I too was able to tell him many times over how much I loved and appreciated him.

Bedridden, looking out his window across the Joshua tree spotted desert to the distant hills, he would spot planes taking off and landing throughout the day and into the evening. It was his final and ultimate joy to see them fly daily. Until the very last day of his life, dad's eyes would light up as he pointed out the window toward the small planes moving through the sky at Fox Airfield in the distance, the joy of flight with him until the very end.

Dad lay at home in his hospital bed, ravaged by cancer, his ailing body in stark contrast to his spirit and the exciting, full life he had led. His eyes, still bright blue, drove deeply into the caverns of my heart as I stood next to him, gazing at his skeletal form. He mustered all his strength requesting a vowed promise from me, "Take care of your mom."

Mom had now spent many long, difficult, weary years nursing and caring for dad but she was still full of feisty, Irish temper, spunk and moxie. We had locked horns on many occasions as I spread my rebellious wings throughout my teen years and into my twenties. Here I stood at my father's death bed and, even still, mom and I had our flaring differences over the care of dad while he was ill, she of course always winning.

Dad had been the peace maker in our relationship all these years and, as I stood grasping the concept of his plea, I wondered how on earth I could ever be the one to take care of Mom, or even more if she would ever allow me or anyone to ever take care of her. Her strength and fortitude was beyond comprehension for me.

Feeling the weight of his request on my heart I took a deep long breath and summoned an answer, looking in his eyes, smiling, hoping that my voice would not betray my doubts or disappoint him. I mustered a doubtful response which came out in a feigned laugh as I gave him a big smile, patted him on the arm telling him, "Mom is far to spunky to need my help. She will be just fine, Dad." His bright blue eyes pierced my soul as he gathered all his waning strength, reaching for my arm, and peered deep inside me seeing a part of me I didn't know existed, stating, "You must promise me you will help her. She needs you. Take care of her. It is up to you now."

It was here at this place in time that I stepped from childhood to womanhood as I accepted his death bed request. Then from my lips and somewhere inside I gave him my heartfelt promise, "Yes Dad, I will do my best to help her as much as I can, as much as she will allow me to. I promise." He nodded approval. We sat for a few minutes in silence as I wondered how I could ever fulfill his wish.

Mom returned to the room and shooed me out. I could not bear to watch her try to get him to take liquid from a spoon as she desperately tried to keep him alive. Suddenly, she was sobbing saying, "No Marty don't leave. Please don't leave." I stepped back into the room next to dad's bed, mom kissed him goodbye and then ran out of the room unable to contain herself. I leaned over him, gave him a kiss, put my arms around him and doubting my words, yet accepting the mantle he placed upon me, I softly whispered, "It's okay Dad. You can go. We are all okay. We will all be okay. I promise."

I literally felt his spirit leave his body. A soft breeze moved by me and then out of the room... out the front door... out of the house. He was gone, heaven bound, finally free of the earthly trappings of suffering and pain. Free at long last to fly, to soar to the heavens.

Dad was my North Star and, to the end, he was strong for me, my brother and most of all for my mother. A Catholic Mass funeral service was held for dad at Sacred Heart Church in Lancaster. Many friends from NACA and NASA from over the years attended. Some of dad's family from Hampton, Virginia, his sister, Aunt Mary, and oldest nephew, Joe, from the East coast flew in for his funeral as well. Grief overcame me at the funeral; my memory is only of a gentleman in attendance who stepped into the isle to catch me and hold me up as I lost the strength to walk, helping me along, supporting me as my legs betrayed my body on the long walk out of the church behind the coffin. The limo ride to the cemetery was a welcome refuge for my pain and my weak rubbery legs.

Dad was honored as an American patriot with a soldier's burial, the American flag draped over his coffin, the cemetery American flag at half mast, along with a fitting, stunning Air Force jet, missing man formation fly-over which took my breath away and drove home the reality of his dreams, his life come to an end. The soldiers saluted dad's coffin and performed a regimented military Flag Folding Ceremony presentation of the coffin flag to mom.

I have no memory of what was said at the funeral just tears, mom's broken heartedness, my brother's lost and lonely pain, our family grief – just absolutes, feelings of finality that I thought would never come and desperately wanted to push away – the deep void and the grief that comes with loosing the family cornerstone, our compass.

Dad left us at only 64 years of age, on October 2, 1982. My parents had been married for 38 years at the time. Mom never remarried, celebrating their wedding anniversary every year. He truly was the one and only true love of her life. No one else could hold a candle to him; even with all his human frailties no one ever measured up to Marty Byrnes.

**For me I hold close the thought that
one day in heaven I will
"dance with my father again."**

*"You can kiss your family and friends goodbye and
put miles between you,
but at the same time you carry them with you
in your heart, your mind, your stomach, because you
do not just live in a world
but a world lives within you."*

*~ Frederick Buechner
Telling The Truth*

Betty Byrnes

Chapter 3

Promise Fulfilled

Loosing dad left mom lonely and lost, taking several years before she rallied through a gamut of emotions to finally begin to travel. She had kept in touch with distant relatives in Ireland and England with her letter correspondence all her life. Finally, she traveled to Ireland, fulfilling a lifelong wish to visit the land of her and dad's heritage, something she had wanted her entire life and had planned to do with dad. He traveled with her in spirit and heart.

She also showed her spunk and vigor when she hopped on board planes and buses alone, traveling across the U.S. to visit her WAC friend, Mary Martin, in Nebraska. Mary had been her bridesmaid all those years ago and stood look out at the Quonset hut door while mom and dad rendezvoused. Mom also returned to upstate New York, where she visited with relatives, showing her love by caring for her ailing sisters and then one by one attended the burials of each, Aunts Elizabeth, Frances and Gertie and then Gertie's husband, Uncle John Spada, who was like a brother to mom. Gertie, like mom, had a forever true love with her husband. After her death Uncle John could not hold on to life without her and followed her to heaven's gates less than a year later, literally dying of a broken heart. Mom the youngest in her family survived all her siblings.

Mom lived a long life to the age of 82 and, true to my word and promise to dad, I took care of her to the end. It was not an easy task. There were many bumps in the road. Our differences in how we approached life were drastic. We were very different people. We butted heads, clashing at every turn just as in my teen years; however I learned she and I shared a very sturdy Irish fortitude to never give up, to pray always and trust God. Our commonality was that we were faith filled survivors.

'One day at a time,' the realization came that as we trudged through life moving forward the tables had turned and God had healed our relationship. Where there had been animosity, frustration and resentment there now lived deep admiration, love and support. Her favorite prayer was the prayer of St. Francis of Assisi which was all over the house. This prayer became a reality in our relationship. Mom had become my very best friend, the needed support reciprocated, the first person I called in any situation as I too was to her.

The last five years of mom's life were an endless struggle of deteriorating health; ironically her very active, sports like body also betrayed her, holding her hostage just as dad's had done. I watched helplessly and worked hard to bring her caregivers who could watch, protect and care for her. Endless infarctions, mini strokes, physically disabled her, ravaged her once active body... yet her brain stayed sharp and alert.

Her biggest wish was for me to gather all the boxes of family pictures dad had taken and collected over the years and place them into a photo album, which had never been done. There were many family gatherings and dinners held at my insistence rounding up grandkids, Dennis and nephews as often as possible. It was important to me that my children be there for their grandmother and know as much about her as possible. We spent many hours poring over the giant family photo album. It was nothing fancy – just dad's lifetime of pictures sorted and organized, finally, which felt like an astronomical feat. Her favorite moments were sharing the photo album with those who visited, whether it be a nurse, a friend or a random visitor. Endless hours were spent flipping through the photos while she shared family stories she'd never previously divulged. This is when I learned of mom and dad's courtship in France during the war. Time with the elderly is a most precious gift. They have so much to share and teach. Mom's grandchildren and great grandchild, Tayler, (there was only one at the time), were blessed to spend time with her, learn from her and share in her care. She so loved having all her family near her. I truly believe our society makes a grave mistake in alienating and minimizing the elderly. They are an important part of teaching the young compassion, patience, history and the cycle of life.

Regular weekly trips to buy groceries, spend time, monitor caregivers, take her shopping turned into precious, treasured moments. We packed up the walker in the beginning and went on outings to the Skunk Works park in Palmdale, where we sat and watched the kids play on airplanes, or took off to the mall, out to eat, or just out grocery shopping. We talked, laughed, argued and cried together. Her illness, much like dad's, moved her from the cane, to the walker to the wheelchair as her health progressively worsened. She fought every declining step with tenacity and determination grasping tight to her dignity and life; however, at the end of each battle she would turn to me and say, "Ok, Betty, if you think it's best" and we would transition her.

We countered every declining step with a positive event taking her out of the house to enjoy something she loved. One outing she particularly enjoyed was to St. Andrews Abby, for Valyermo Fall Fair in September 1999. This was a typical Catholic fair with lots of food, crafts and the traditional free flowing beer. Mom's eyes twinkled enjoying her beer as the starring act, The Singing Nuns, performed lively renditions of many '50s and '60s Pop songs, evoking waves of fun nostalgia and uproarious applause from the crowd.

However, her biggest wish was to visit the Kern River where she had spent so many vacations over the decades with the family and then just with dad and Ginger after we grew and left home. This would be the last vacation place I would be privileged to take mom. Her final sweet wish was to one more time smell the Kern pine trees, hear the soothing roar of the rapids and feel the coolness of the river water on her feet, saying "I just want to dunk my feet in the Kern River one more time." We made the long, familiar winding drive up the mountain to the Kern with the wheel chair and ice chest in the trunk for a day trip. There in her and dad's favorite camping spot on the Kern, Headquarters Campground, she was able to dunk her feet in the river water. It had been years since I'd been to this particular campsite and was very pleased to see that handicap cement areas had been installed. Disappointedly though, I was unable to wheel mom all the way down to the river but, thanks to the handicap areas, was able to get her very close and then, I hauled up water to her from the river in a large camping bowl I'd by chance brought along. We took off her shoes and she felt the cool river water on her toes. It was so lovely to see her smile. We sat by the river relaxed, listened to the birds and rapids, barbecued hamburgers and hot dogs.

All the while, I watched as mom's mind drifted to some previous time in her life. She was happy. Dad had blessed me beyond measure holding me to the promise to care for mom. Yes, she needed me; however I needed her so much more. It was my honor, joy and privilege to keep my promise to dad. I cared for Mom until the last moment of her life.

Mother lived another 18 years after dad passed away, passing on March 31, 2000. She never lost that spunk, vigor and tenacity, the bedrock of her personality, the inherent qualities which forged the strong Army nurse and NASA wife she was. Dad provided for her and she retired comfortably, keeping busy for many years, bringing little tokens of love to her grandchildren and children... always thrifty and frugal, many of them from the thrift store where she volunteered endless hours. So many times, we'd think they were silly or didn't care for them much; yet now they have become precious treasured memories of her love. She also personally delivered care packages to the needy via St. Vincent de Paul. She would worry Dennis and I as she traveled into neighborhoods the police were even wary of to deliver boxes of food and clothes to the needy. Her eyes would shine as she shared with me how she loved to hold the new babies when she dropped off food. That was her payment for her devotion to the needy. She spent her time, gas and money on others throughout her neighborhood and community, giving them rides and helping wherever needed. She generously sponsored and privately paid for private Catholic school through scholarships she set up at Sacred Heart Church in Lancaster, enabling a needy child each year to receive a private quality education. I was flabbergasted to learn when I took over her finances she had been donating to a seemingly endless list of charities for many years. Dad and mom's favorites at the top were the St. Joseph's

Indian School and Missions and Maryknoll Catholic missions. She never openly spoke of these donations but that was her way and dad's way as they were raised, biblically taught not to speak of helping others so as not to boast or take credit for good works, but to help out of love of others and the Lord.

Just as for dad, a Catholic Mass funeral service was performed for mom. I had held things together for her for many years, but planning the funeral was exceptionally hard for me. No matter how ill a beloved family member is, no matter how you prepare mentally or emotionally for the inevitable death, you can never plan how your grief will grip you in the end. Although I'd preplanned and discussed with mom how she wanted her service to go, I regret to this day that I failed to arrange for her favorite song to be sung, "Oh Danny Boy". By the time I remembered it was too late and the pianist and vocalist did not have time to get the music. Here I post that song in her honor, hearing clearly in my mind dad's beautiful clear tenor voice singing it for her. Many people attended her funeral. I was amazed at the number of people I had never met who approached me and told me how kind and giving my mother was, sharing heartfelt personal stories of her kindness, how she had touched their lives, made it better for them in some simple but meaningful way, how she had helped so many over the years. There were friends from NACA and NASA present, who shared happy fond memories of mom or funny stories about her spunkiness. It was so wonderful to see my parent's friends I grew up around also present to honor her and say goodbye.

The city gave her a police escort for the funeral procession from the church to the cemetery, something I had not planned nor was told about prior, the sirens blaring as mom rolled through the town of Lancaster one last time. I thought it was so fitting for her feisty spirit; however, we all laughed through our tears at how much mom who was so low key and frugal would not have wanted such an expense or such attention. She was buried in the family plot near dad and my sister Patty. She was also given a patriot's military burial, acknowledging the years she honorably served her country, the American flag draped over her coffin just as it had been done for dad. The cemetery American flag stood at half mast. It was a surreal, almost out of body experience to be burying my mother as the soldiers played Taps, performed the Funeral Flag Folding Ceremony and crisply saluted her coffin. Then, they sharply turned and presented the triangle shaped flag to me.

Numbly I felt my hands reach out and gratefully accept it then placed it on my lap. Dennis was a Vietnam War Veteran and my heart broke for him as he, too, was racked by grief. I held the flag close for a while during mom's graveside service and then handed the flag to him. He of all people needed and would appreciate mom's burial flag even more than myself, as he had served his country and knew the price paid to receive the honor of a military funeral. The look of gratitude on his face confirmed it all to me.

Where dad had been my North Star, mom had been my bedrock. I simply could not imagine life without her. Through the ups and downs of our lives mom and I had become the very closest of friends. She had suffered from over four years of a debilitating disease which increasingly ravaged her body, robbing her of the freedom to move. She passed away at home with her family around her in the very same room as dad had. After his death, she had moved into that room and slept there all those following years, the same room where she last kissed dad goodbye. It was there where she also said her last goodbyes and whispered to me that dad was there. I had been strong for her. I had kept my promise to dad. She looked me in the eyes and I saw gratitude and love. I told her one last time her how much I loved her and kissed her. Her last words to me were, "This will be the hardest on you." Then she passed away. I know that Dad was there to meet her.

I wasn't sure what mom meant by that at first. She knew what it meant to be strong. I had been strong for her and for my children for a very long time... just as she had been so strong for dad and for us, with her death came a huge void. I was forced to stop and take a breath... consumed and alone in grief. It was then I realized what she meant. When you no longer need to be strong... that is when the avalanche of pain comes. In retrospect I see how God carried me through so much and fulfilled his word in my life. God truly was my strength through it all.

"I can do all things through Christ who strengthens me." ~ Philippians 4:13

Trust in the LORD with all your heart and lean not on your own understanding; in all your ways acknowledge him, and he will make your paths straight.
~ Proverbs 3:5-6

*"Walking. I am listening to a deeper way.
Suddenly all my ancestors are behind me.
Be still, they say. Watch and listen.
You are the result of the love of thousands."*

~ Linda K. Hogan, Native American Writer

Chapter 4

Mom's Last Gift

There had been over four years of full-time caregivers and nurses for mom. At one juncture, there had been a call from one care giver. This was when she was still able to walk with her walker. Losing her independence, of course, never sat well with her. She railed against the confinements of being watched and cared for. In her typical independent spirit she broke free from the caregiver, making her way into the master bedroom and belligerently shut the door, locked it and ordered her to stay out. The caregiver, a conscientious, loving nurse from Belize, spent much time pleading and prompting her to allow her in but was unable to persuade her to open the locked door or come out of the room. Greatly concerned for her safety, she called me at work sounding panicked. At this time, my mother's mind was still very sharp, but her body was increasingly giving out. I had given explicit instructions to all the caregivers never to leave her alone as she had a tendency to fall and needed someone present 24/7. Asking her to pass the phone to my mother so I could decipher why she was locked in the master bedroom, mom relented, unlocked the door long enough to take the phone and talk to me.

Barely audible in her delayed speech, which increasingly slowed throughout her illness, she whispered into the receiver, "I... I... I... can't... talk. I'm... busy. I'm... taking care... of business." I had no clue what she meant, but she promised me she would finish up and let the caregiver in. Letting some time pass, I then called back to verify mom had kept her word, opened the door and allowed the caregiver access again. She had. I chalked it up to just needing to have some personal space, alone time, as she was still adjusting to losing her privacy now that she was being monitored 24/7.

Although she slept in dad's final room after he passed away, many of her personal belongings, including her mahogany dressers, were still in the master bedroom, each with their personal items still in the original designated spots, the very first assigned spots as the day my parents newly married. No matter where we moved, the knickknacks and personal items on mom and dad's dressers remained exactly in the very same specific places. Today, I know this brought mom a sense of order, continuity and stability as a result of our nomadic lives. No matter what rental or house we lived in, if her things were in the same place we were 'home'.

Mom always placed her wedding picture, the musical powder box, her pin box and other odds and ends precisely so. I also knew exactly where they each sat because for years it had been my chore to dust and oil the furniture throughout the house. Each item had to be placed where it had been originally placed by mom. Just at the right angle and stance. Dad had been the same way too, apparently a throwback to regimented Army days. On one of my weekly visits about a month earlier, I noticed many of her items in the master bedroom were moved and gone. I searched through her drawers, thinking maybe someone cleaned and stored them away, only to discover some had been stolen by caregivers from agencies we no longer used... for good reason. My heart had sank when I realized they had gone through her things and taken them. I decided not to say a word to her about the theft as I knew it would break her heart.

On my next visit after the panicked phone call, I examined the bedroom again and realized mom's wedding picture and some other items were also gone and there was now little left on her dresser. Again completely heartbroken and trying to protect her and not cause drama I decided not to say a word to her. Looking further it was hard to tell why she had locked herself in the room except to just get some private time so I attempted to talk to her about the incident, but all she would whisper is, "It's all taken care of." She had her reasons and seemed to just want privacy. Putting it into perspective and looking at the larger picture there was always so much to accomplish on my visits along with my main focus which was spending quality time with her... I just let it go.

Upon her death, the dark mahogany bedroom set became my son's. Dennis had moved it to my home and I was cleaning out the sturdy dresser drawers, setting it up in Justin's room, amazed at how well taken care of it was. It was almost 60 years old and like brand new; albeit better made than most furniture today. As I reached into the very back of dad's bottom dresser drawer to clear it, I felt something unusual under several layers of dry-cleaner plastic which mom had used to line the drawers. Chuckling, I thought about how she never threw much of anything away but always looked for ways to save and reuse almost everything, a habit she had acquired living through the depression. Curiously, I felt something unusually odd in my hand. Carefully pulling it out, I wondered what on earth it could be. There nestled and squirreled away, wrapped in multiple layers of old dry-cleaning plastic was mom and dad's wedding picture in the original glass and mahogany frame.

The art deco picture frame had come as a gift with the bedroom set. The wedding picture that had sat in the same spot on her dresser for nearly 60 years. As I slowly unwrapped the plastic, revealing the lost treasure in my hand, time stood still. I felt her touch on my shoulder, heard her words, "I'm taking care of business." Holding my parent's, lost forever, wedding picture in my hands, I wept as I saw her smile one more time, just as I had seen her do so many times over the decades as she walked past the picture... a glance, a memory, a smile. She had hidden her treasure, her heart. My mother's very last, eternal gift to me, a simple wedding picture in an art deco frame ...

representing the love they shared for all those many years.

Betty Byrnes

Moon Child: Growing Up NASA

*Oh, Danny boy, the pipes, the pipes are calling

From glen to glen, and down the mountain side

The summer's gone, and all the flow'rs are dying

'Tis you, 'tis you must go and I must bide.

But come ye back when summer's in the meadow

Or when the valley's hushed and white with snow

'Tis I'll be here in sunshine or in shadow

Oh, Danny boy, oh, Danny boy, I love you so.

And if you come, and all the flowers are dying

If I am dead, as dead I well may be

I pray you'll find the place where I am lying

And kneel and say an "Ave" there for me.

And I shall hear, though soft you tread above me

And all my grave will warm and sweeter be

And then you'll kneel and whisper that you love me

And I shall sleep in peace until you come to me.

* "Oh Danny Boy" song is a ballad written by English songwriter Frederic Weatherly and usually set to the Irish tune of the "Londonderry Air".

Betty Byrnes

Part 6

Conclusion

Everything Comes Full Circle

"If there is any period one would desire to be born in, is it not the age of Revolution; when the old and the new stand side by side... when the glories of the old can be compensated by the rich possibilities of the new era? This time... is a very good one."

~ Ralph Waldo Emerson

The following are several journal notes I kept while experiencing landmark moments in NASA history with my father's spirit by my side.

August 5, 2012

The same day Curiosity has landed on Mars a surreal feeling came over me as I typed up and documented my father's life with NASA via his memoirs simultaneously watching and cheering on NASA as the brilliant engineers jubilantly achieved a precise spot-on landing of a second rover on Mars. I know in my heart dad would have so loved to be a part of this, yet I know he is watching from heaven's gates.

September 17, 2012

Today marks the end of an era in my life, my father's and for NASA, the mothership. It has been 12 years since my mother's passing, 30 years since my father's passing and 50 years since my dad first embarked on his journey with NASA. The space program as I grew up with it, evolving through time from NACA to NASA; Mercury, Gemini, Apollo and ultimately the Space Shuttle... is over.

During the writing of this book, a second Land Rover, Curiosity, landed on Mars, the Space Shuttle, Endeavor, "The Regal Work Horse" has been retired to the California Science Center. Neil Armstrong, the first moonwalker, has passed away and now moon walks beyond the moon and the stars taking his heavenly place for all eternity. I know my dad was there to greet him at heaven's gates and, yes, I go out often and give a wink at the moon for both Neil Armstrong and my dad.

This day I woke early, which is not the norm for me any longer. I am 61 and retired now. Many years have passed since the little girl who held on tight to her daddy looked up into the sky to wave at our neighbor, Scott Crossfield, the X-15 test pilot, as he flew over head in the bright blue, California desert sky. Yet, I can still feel my dad's touch and presence. I know without a doubt that today I need to be somewhere very special. This is a landmark day in space history.

This morning with great anticipation I stand on the dry, desert earth in Palmdale, California, the sister city to Lancaster where I spent the first 7 years of my life as a NACA / NASA child. Here on the high desert streets of Palmdale, overlooking Dryden Research Center and the Antelope Valley, I stand gazing anxiously out into the vast, blue morning sky. There are others gathering around me. Everyone is friendly and the energy is high in anticipation of seeing the Space Shuttle Endeavor on her very last flight. As with all space flights this is not just a once-in-a-lifetime event but a one-time-in-history flight. Here the crown jewel will fly again, not by the power of rocket boosters into space but piggy back on a NASA 747 airship, which after this historic trip will also be retired to Edwards Air Force Base museum. Today, inexplicably, magnetically, I have been pulled here to this place, my Dad's spirit accompanies me in a way I have not felt for many years. I feel his presence deeply today. I know without a doubt I am in God's perfect place in time.

I have pulled off the road at a high spot which overlooks the Antelope Valley floor and close to the hangars of Dryden, where all five of the Space

Shuttles completed the building process over the years, the first Space Shuttle completed being the Enterprise. This is the same place where dad last worked for NASA on the Space Shuttle Enterprise before his illness and death, the place which brought completeness and joy back into his life, the place where he was 'back in the airplane business'. Today Space Shuttle Endeavor will flyover this spot and acknowledge all those whose hard work made NASA a success. I knew in my heart I had to be here to represent for dad.

There is a strong breeze as always in Palmdale today. The temp a pleasant 75 degrees with a slight haze laying low to the ground, which we all regretfully determine to be smog. I remember a time when smog in this valley was unheard of. As I gaze out over the valley floor which stretches for endless unobstructed miles, a graceful, rainbow colored, hot air balloon delicately floats. As the obvious juxtaposition settles in, I openly make the statement, "Now that is the perfect place, perfect way to view the final journey of Endeavor." Longing to be in the basket of that beauty, a friendly lady next to me, a stranger, hands me her binoculars so I can get a better look at the exquisite delicacy of the hot air balloon. I gratefully accept them and peer through the lenses as a history lesson of flight flashes through my mind. The balloon elicits memories of dad's love of the Wright Brothers and the magic of Dad's love of flight reaches somewhere deep inside.

Traveling through time and then back to where I stand wonderful warm memories of his smile and laughter fill my heart, his pervasive essence surrounds me. The vision of his face fills my mind... his eyes as he looked off into space while sitting behind President Kennedy at Rice Stadium told the story of a journey fulfilled long before the first

Mercury space launch... this same look is what I see... the sheer love of flight.

A ginormous cheer goes up jolting me back to the present. We all point and cheer as we see a speck at first in the distance, ironically just beyond the hot air balloon, then larger and larger as it begins its wide looping approach to Dryden Research Center with the huge 747's first powerful swoop, flying abnormally low across the desert floor. We are all dumbfounded and mesmerized at the sheer beauty as it slowly glides by right in front of us, Endeavor sitting pristinely, majestically on top.

The intrinsic grandeur of these two in flight leaves us awestruck. It's colossal presence, the sheer massiveness of Endeavor now very apparent, defying gravity yet one more time. Before us, the gigantic ship smoothly glides directly over the Dryden hangars like a mammoth, elegant creature of the sky. I am expecting this ship's sound to be very loud but it is powerfully quiet, which leaves the crowd in a reverential hush. My heart leaps out of my chest and I have chills all over my body. This is it! I can feel my dad's presence and see the excitement in his face from years gone by. Memories of his joy from the many trips out to carriers for Mercury flights and trips to the neighboring Mojave Desert floor for Space Shuttle landings. This is it! This is what he felt!

Endeavor, the last of the Space Shuttles will ultimately be housed at the California Science Center, Samuel Oschin Display Pavilion, Exposition Park in Los Angeles. I will visit there, but this monumental day... she is regally airborne for one last glorious flight.

This day, oh so fittingly, Endeavor upon approach to Dryden in Palmdale, as if in salute to both dad and mom and also to Walt Williams, dad's boss all those many loyal years – made her approach from the direction of Lancaster where they all now lay at rest.

Feeling the low-pitched, powerful engines of the huge airship before me all the way down to my toes, I tilt my head back, chin up, eyes to the sky. It seemed I could just reach up and touch her as they hung in the air before me. Magnificently gliding very low across the bright blue California sky, Endeavor paid homage to the men and women at Dryden Research Center with two flyovers. Unanticipated emotions hit me hard. It was as if a damn opened and tears began to flow. There before me flew the culmination of all dad's dreams, his hard work, his 'endeavors' for so many decades come to complete fruition and closure. The finality hit me.

As I stood there enveloped in thought, overcome with feeling, a lady approached saying, "You too? My dad worked on the Space Shuttle. You look like you could use a hug." No explanations needed, a bear hug and tears flowing. Two strangers brought together by God for just this moment in time. We quickly learned that NASA and space flight were the hub of our family life. We had both grown up around 'space flight', lived in the Antelope Valley, both 'desert rats', visited the Kern River as children and adults, experienced the roar of jets passing over head at a personal level, our fathers' love of flight and space the key integral part of our families. We both stood together on the California desert floor acknowledging an era is over on so many levels. We both agreed our fathers would be proud of us as we stood there publicly expressing acknowledgment of their hard work and their hand in NASA history.

Saying goodbye to my new friends I left Palmdale, hopped in my car and drove over an hour on the crazy California freeways in bumper to bumper traffic forging my way to the Griffith Park Observatory to see the venerable vessel in flight one last time. It was so very well worth the journey. Endeavor still securely and grandly perched atop the skillfully flown 747 for this last celebratory flight had left us in Palmdale, made her way up the California coastline and then down south. She flew over many landmarks and throngs of cheering crowds.

Leaving Dryden in Palmdale she flew on to Sacramento, acknowledging the capitol, then over to San Francisco where she magnificently passed over the Golden Gate Bridge, progressed south down the Pacific shores, over Point Magu Naval Base and on to Malibu. Making her approach to L.A from the Santa Monica Pier, the Hollywood Sign and Griffith Park Observatory. Finally then over downtown Los Angeles, and ultimately, in jubilant ceremony landing at Los Angeles International Airport. There, as the pilot taxied down the runway to a special holding hangar, he displayed the beautiful American flag out of the top hatch of the plane which gallantly rippled in the breeze for all the world to see. This was the cherry on the cake buoying great cheers and chants of, "USA! USA! USA!" from the ecstatic, singing crowds and marching band.

It was at Griffith Park Observatory where she flew directly over the spot where I now stood in the park's high scrub brush covered hills. I had climbed up a hill just off the road to garner the best vantage point. By this time, literally thousands of people lined the streets and hills filling the park and forcing the closure of all roads. God's perfect timing allowed me access to a very close parking space where I claimed my dusty, scrub-brush perch just moments before the roads were closed.

People from all generations and nationalities were cheering and smiling, simply amazed to be present for this once in a life time moment, an epic juncture birthed from simpler and gentler times. A deeply patriotic age when emphatic pride of God, country and family ran deep in the veins of the nation... a time when the revered U.S. flag stood for freedom, all that was right and good, cherished and held dear. There I stood with these same feelings still rooted deep within as Endeavor made not one but two passes over Griffith Park Observatory and the Hollywood Sign, relishing one last time that, again, I was that little girl in the field in my Daddy's arms hearing his words, "Look up, Betty Bean! Look up! You'll see it fly by!" That I did... for as long as possible, chin up, head tilted back and mouth open... watching until Endeavor now accompanied by two beautiful white escort jets slowly became just a dot in the sky and disappeared... deep pride, love of God, family and country burning in my heart. My father and mother gave me that. NASA gave us that. The pride I feel as the daughter of Martin A. Byrnes Jr. remains strong and will always be my family's, my children's and grand children's legacy for all generations to come.

October 14, 2012

Another momentous day in Endeavor history at Exposition Park with the majestic Endeavor. She has now slowly inch by inch and foot by foot traveled the streets of Los Angeles from LA International Airport to Exposition Park, her final retirement home. News sources say over a million people have hit the streets to view Endeavor on her final journey. The crowd whose eyes are all focused on the stately, gigantic, flying machine let out spontaneous cheers of joy along with chants of "USA! USA! USA!" at various times.

Today, I made my way to Exposition Park to see the regal vessel, Endeavor, arrive. To garner an up close and personal view of her in her very last transport movements. A huge gathering made it difficult to politely maneuver to the front where I knew I needed to be to gain a better view. I move carefully, forging slowly forward inch by inch. Yes, the crowd is large but there is a collective, respectful silence. A very real, discernible, tangible sense of awe filled the air, blanketed the crowd. A respectful awareness for space history, as well as the living history we were all experiencing in the moment. Quiet, yet excited conversations were shared between complete strangers about space and shuttle Endeavor facts. Children asked questions and were eager to learn. I love to see the light in a child's eyes as they experience learning. Yes, this is the perfect place for Endeavor's final home. Here, today, the children were drinking in, absorbing history in the making, enkindling imagination, working her magic, continuing to teach, bringing space history to future generations. Here, in this place, she will be the conduit to ignite the fire for space travel in the hearts of the country's future astronauts and space engineers.

Everyone from all nationalities and languages were polite and accommodating, even helpful, allowing others to move to the front of the crowd to gain closer pictures, then moving out to make way for others. Once, a tall man with a better view happily took several cameras, filming and snapping pics for others. The crowd was indeed impressive and memorable. How often in life do you see a multitude of all nationalities come together so respectfully and peacefully? Endeavor and NASA accomplished this.

You simply cannot look at Endeavor's massiveness and splendor without feeling the awe that emanates from her. She is proudly cloaked with thousands of miles of space wear, little meteorite tings, dings, nudges and blastoff coloration regale her outer shell.

Looking at her beckons a vision of the thousands of men and women who made her journey to space and back, then to this very moment in time, possible... including my father and his fellow coworkers. The brilliant, gifted, motivated people. The astronauts who logged thousands of meticulous hours of space task work inside her walls. Performing astonishing feats tethered and propelled outside her boundaries floating in the dark of space with only the company of twinkling stars.

The NASA space program has not only brought us Teflon, Tang, memory foam, satellite TV, UV sunglasses, clear braces and the IPOD (to name just a few NASA research discoveries) but displayed the cohesive magnetic patriotic force I grew up with. As if laying in wait a yearning, a need to express a deeply rooted common spirit has only needed Endeavor to draw people from their homes and launch them to the streets and hills, voices raised. I personally have not seen this sort of patriotism since the first space flights of Mercury in the early 1960's. Thousands flocked to the streets en masse to stand in awe and wonder. People converged on hilltops, piers, bridges, roof tops and in the streets of California over the last two months to view Endeavor's unforgettable final historic, magnificent journey. People from all levels of society flocking toward one goal, with one mind set... to view her final flyover atop the NASA 747... then to be apart of her historic slow 2 mph trek on earth as she is slowly and precisely edged and maneuvered over the streets of Los Angeles. The magnificent flying machine which traveled through space at speeds of 17,500mph now moving at 2mph. Unfathomable, unimaginable in either state.

Standing for hours gazing at Endeavor, my mind traveled back to my childhood, the beginning days of Mercury, Gemini and Apollo.... growing up NASA. Then, it fast forwarded, remembering the humble look of joy on my father's face after his retirement as he showed me pictures of the time he and mom were invited as a VIP guests to watch the Shuttle landings in the Mojave desert. He was there from inception to the end of the program he helped start. In my heart, I know how happy and blessed he would be to know I was representing for him today... for everything in life comes full circle.

November 11, 2012

My son, Justin, his good friend, Jarrod, and myself visit Exposition Park Space Museum in downtown Los Angeles to see up close and personal the Endeavor Space Shuttle inside her final hangar. It was simply an amazing day! To stand directly under this majestic vessel... mind boggling. The Space Museum had hands-on displays of Mercury, Gemini and Apollo capsules as well as astronaut space suits and space equipment for viewing. However, the cherry on the cake was the elegant Endeavor which held us transfixed and mesmerized for hours. We could barely pull ourselves away.

How can it be that an inanimate object can have such a glow even in its space worn underbelly? It is simply the most amazing piece of machinery ever made by man. We spent many hours looking at this regal vessel, examining it's under belly, the giant engines, the space tinged and dinged outside adding even more character. Justin and his friend tell me today was better than their first trip to Disneyland when they were small. The grins on their faces and the joy in their eyes affirm their statement. Yes, the love of space runs deep in the family continuing from generation to generation. It is a simply euphoric unforgettable day witnessing up close and personal this unique and special part of U.S. space history. What a privilege to know our family legacy is so closely linked, so much a part of it. Thank you, Dad, for all your brilliant, visionary, hard work.

"Dare to live the life you have dreamed for yourself. Go forward and make your dreams come true."

~ Ralph Waldo Emerson

Betty Byrnes

MEMOIRS by
MARTIN A. BYRNES JR. 1917 – 1982

~~~~~~~~~~~~~~~~~~~~~~~~

As I wrote this book, nearing the end, I began to type up dad's memoirs which he had been compiling for many years. His coworker and friend, Sr. Engineer, Gene Matranga, from Dryden Research Center in Palmdale had visited with him at home and had encouraged him to document his time with NASA. Sadly he was never able to finish his work as illness gripped his life.

It simply was impossible to accomplish finishing his project as I am not qualified to attempt to give scientific data or historic details as he would have. Yet I knew that the Lord was guiding me. Not believing in coincidences I fully felt that somehow I had been given an assignment, a mission to complete dad's journey with NASA via Moon Child: Growing Up NASA. As a result I was led to write this book of NASA through the eyes of a small child's love of her father as a legacy for my family for generations to come.

My father began his notes for a book in the late '70s intending to cover his career from NACA throughout NASA years. This is a capsulation of his memoirs, although incomplete and sporadic they hold much detailed information and criteria on his findings, experience and the process of the behind the scenes space flight drama during a ground breaking time in history.

After my mother's death I discovered dad's memoirs and many boxes of original pictures of Edwards and the NASA Space Research Center in Houston, from ground breaking forward. In this treasure trove are detailed outlines and notes allowing a glimpse at a computer-less day and age when only the brilliance of the human mind put pen to paper accomplishing giant feats. He explains the plans of the NASA Space Task Group (STG) which was formed to complete President Kennedy's moon space mission. Included are stories and criteria for Dad's assigned visits and research on many possible NASA locations which led to the deciding factor of Houston, Texas as NASA's home base. There are anecdotes and remembrances of astronauts, space flights, trips on carriers and his experience at making the final call to allow Gus Grissom's capsule, Liberty Bell 7, sink to the bottom of the Atlantic Ocean.

The following are writings... just as I found them, unfinished memoirs, anecdotes and notes from Martin A. Byrnes Jr., the first manager of NASA Space Research Center:

Part I
Flight Testin' is Fun

Much has been written about the exciting period at the beginning of the era of the supersonic aircraft and its phasing forward at an ever accelerating pace into the space age. This period of our national growth has produce many serious first-hand reports both objective and personal. This progress we shaped in the days for the X-1 through X-15, and beyond through Project Mercury, had room for a lighter side which really rounds out the portrait of the kind of men who got us from the biplane into space.

In Walter Williams' office, now at Aerospace Corporation in El Segundo hangs a caricature of a test pilot. It is the face of a grizzly old sourdough desert prospector set in a Lombard flight helmet with shoulders clad in a pressure suit. The caption is "Flight Testin' is Fun". It is a smaller copy of a large version which used to hang in the Officers Club at Edwards Air Force Base, the Flight Test Center for Advanced military and civilian aircraft since the first days of the F-80 when that very hush-hush new airplane was sheltered in a carefully guarded hangar area at the old North Base.

The high morale, rare good humor, the occasional practical jokes and horseplay were characteristic of the hard-working, hard-playing flight test teams, test pilots and support crews alike. The desert location known in the late 1940's as Muroc, with its fabulously large natural flying field, Rogers Dry Lake, was ideal for flight test work but in spite of the good humored G.I. type complaining it was really a pretty terrible place to live until some of the trimmings such as air-conditioning could be added during the 1950's. But high morale, espirit de corps and intense interest in the fantastic possibilities of the tasks at hand carried Muroc Army Air Base through its dedication as Edwards Air Force Base to distinction in the history of the world.

One comment by an early "desert rat" at Edwards serves to point up the wry good humor of the crews of those days. Mid afternoon, temperature 110° F or thereabouts, Fergie and I were hastening along the narrow straight paved ribbon of a road to Mojave to pick up an official visitor from the railroad station. Suddenly he turned his gaze from the shimmering road ahead and said with a broad grin, "They say you live longer out here. That's a damned lie. It just seems longer."

The same across-the-desert drives in the mid-afternoon heat happened frequently in the process of getting the job done. In the first week after I arrived at Muroc in 1949 some necessary changes in the design of the battery shop being built as an extension to the work area beside the old East Butler hangar occupied by NACA's Flight Test Unit on the Muroc Main Base required the pick-up of some special plumbing materials in Lancaster 30 miles away. Passing the word that a "Lancaster Pick-up" was about to take place, people began to remember that there were other things "urgently" needed so I left the base in the trusty government Ford station wagon with a sizable list.

I arrived in Lancaster about 10:45 to discover that nearly all of the supply places I had to deal with closed from 11:00 to 1:00 for lunch. About 3:00 p.m. I left Lancaster with a very overloaded Ford sagging along between Lancaster's outlying irrigated alfalfa fields at about 40 m.p.h. As the hour long trip wore on and the 100° + heat bore down, my anxiety over tortured tires holding out for another 15-20 mile of hot road and a general feeling of "Please, Mr. Custer" had really closed in on me. Then suddenly, as I glanced to the right toward the brown and red buttes to the East, there across the desert brush about a mile and half away, majestically stood a full scale battleship. I was immediately convinced that I'd had it, the desert heat had finally got me. What I saw in truth, I found out later, was a World War II bomb target made of framing and camouflage net, a replica of a Japanese dreadnought. I made it back to the base without loosing a tire.

Most of the NACA group lived in the Navel housing at the old Air Training Station in Mojave. Most of our flights with the X-1 and the D-558 Phase II were scheduled very early in the morning when the temperature was low and the flying conditions were best -- free of heat and convection problems. The workday was set-up for this reason during the summer months of 1949 as 5:30 a.m. to 2:30 p.m., splendid for early flying but hell-on-wheels for the trip home. Five of us rode in a riding combination so each of our ancient crates only had to survive the afternoon test once a week. From the NACA hangar to the town of Muroc was about 4 1/2 miles. The whole trip to Mojave was about 25 miles by the time we reached Muroc the temperature gage in my nine-year-old 1940 Chevy was pegged at the top of the scale. It stayed there too, until, in the shade behind the apartment with engine still running, I'd raise the hood, push the radiator cap around with a rake handle until it blasted sky high in a rusty geyser of radiator water and steam. Then I'd jam a running water hose into the radiator and let hose and engine run until the gauge indicated the old girl was cooling down.

Part II
Space Challenge – Sputnik

"Where are you Space Yank?"
Fishing trip with Den
Sputnik
Army ready – DOD holdback
NASA: (NACA) philosophy – What was in the stable?
Shapes – X15 extension – Dynosoar
Manned Aircraft Systems Timeline 1923 through 1963

Part III
Suddenly Mercury

Early in the development of the STG the need for new talent was obvious and Bob Gilruth and his staff, having been made aware of a program cancellation at AVRO up in Canada, had been given the opportunity to go to Toronto and interview / select the "cream of the crop" in their close out for STG candidates. The selection / acceptance process produced 28 Canadian and British fellows who reported for duty at Langley. and of this group, one is impressed that a great deal of Project Mercury leadership, among them Jim Chamberlin, was head of the Mercury Engineering Office at the old STG. Later he was Project Manager for Gemini during its early stages. John Hodge was a key man as Flight Director for the Bermuda station. He had to take over the "Go" or "No Go" decision if the spacecraft overflew the Cape's command and tracking capability before the decision was made. Owen Maynard was project engineer on the Apollo Lunar Excursion Module when I left Houston.

Recently John Hodge, Rodney Rose, George Watts, Peter Armitage, David Brown, Morris Jenkins, Thomas Chambers and John Meson and their wives all took the final naturalization step and became U.S. Citizens.

Up until the winter of 1959 the build-up of the Mercury activities at the Cape had been nearly all technical. In the fall we had hired one or two administrative and clerical people other than typists.

In early 1960 I wrote a memo for Gilruth's signature which appointed an acting Administrative Officer for Mercury Cape Activities. I became the first appointee and arranged the STG Contracting Officer, Financial Management Officer and Personnel Officer to set up their functions on an interim basis. Each hired a local office representative in his own way. Harold Collins was hired by Glenn Bailey to be the local contracting officer looking at McDonnell-Mercury Cape activities and providing local purchasing support. Mrs. Mary Driver was transferred in from the STG Langley personnel office.

The Financial Management Officer, Jack Donovan, decided to handle only payroll activities at the Cape but to continue disbursement from Langley. So he had a locally hired finance clerk trained at Langley to keep the unit time clerks' paperwork looking correct when it arrived to Langley. Believe it or not, we never had a late payroll, even though we had some close calls.

Walt Williams had decided the Operations office would have to shift from Langley to Patrick for about two weeks time during each launch. So we had to prepare an office at Patrick.

(Mercury support build-up. Harrington Brown Arbick)

The MA-1 launch in July seemed a good time to take the families to the Cape area. Vacation was a natural for the kids and so Walt and I took our broods with us via Route 17 to the sunny land of Florida. We settled in at the old Tradewinds Hotel in Indiatlantic near the beach on July 24th, five days before launch date. Tom Dougherty, the volatile and generous owner of the Tradewinds, provided a cottage for each family at less than regular cost. To make a short story of it, the weather really blew the whole deal. It rained for 20 days straight. We prolonged count on MA-1 with numerous delays. It rained heavily most of the time. On the morning of the launch, July 29th, you couldn't see the Cape from Cocoa Beach.

High on the scale of happy memories would be the fact that Howard Williams and Denny Byrnes, both age 11, fed up with staying indoors took to the beach and enjoyed getting extremely wet and sandy. During breaks in the rain they would take an old bucket and some of their Dad's fishing tackle and try their luck in the surf which was only a couple of blocks from the cottage area. I had showed Den how to catch a little nickel size shellfish which Floridians called sand fleas and which make good bait for surf fishing. One day just prior to their Dad's return to the household from work at the Cape, the two of them came back from the beach with a whole bucket full of sand fleas, live, and took the crawling mass into our cottage. You guessed it, the eleven year old boy is completely predictable. If anything awkward can happen, it will. The bucket "got tipped over". Hell hath no fury like two wives caged up for days who suddenly find that the family quarters are carpeted with hundreds of swiftly crawling, wet, sandy, beetle-sized shellfish.

We determined that aside from the quarters available at Hangar S at the Cape, there should be a MERCURY Headquarters Office at Patrick to maintain the posture of equal and opposite interface with General Yates' DOD Mercury Office. There was also the presence of the NASA office of Mel Gough in Building No. 425 with General Yates headquarters which no longer formed the main NASA link with the Range except for programs other than Mercury.

The Base Commander allocated the first floor of Building 575 to these civilian upstarts from Mercury and we moved in with vigor in 1960. We painted the place, laid asphalt tile, set up an office comparable to General Don Yates' quarters in Bldg 425 with a conference room graced by a large conference table and twenty-four high back GSA supply service executive chairs. The twenty foot long conference table was designed exactly like the ones in the main conference rooms in NASA's Headquarters and at Langley, we established a reception area graced by attractive Florida decorative plants and a receptionist. The building was not one of the most desirable on the base obviously. However, parking was plentiful and while we were just to the right of the approach flight path of the main runway, the north end of the building faced the aircraft approach path and the south bound traffic on Highway A1A, the main route from the Cape South. Morale was running high and the enthusiasm for the monumental Mercury task was so great that we charged ahead with things which in other more somber and business-as-usual times we probably would do at a slower and more considered pace.

There appeared to be a need to identify this big thing in which we were engaged and give it a public sense of location. I talked with Walt Williams and John Powers and we decided to place easily recognizable labels both at our Cape operation at Hangar S and at Patrick. I talked to Harold Collins the Space Task Group contracting officer at Hangar S and we arranged to have made two signs each consisting of the circular NASA seal, 8 feet in diameter and a proportionate blue strip with white lettering spelling out Project Mercury. The contract included installation. The signs were installed with dispatch one on the front of Hangar S at the Cape and the other mounted on the north wall of Bldg. 575 at Patrick.

There is of course as on any Air Force Base a ground rule that signs and other decorations are not mounted on Air Force buildings without going through the Air Installations Office. Within an hour of our sign installation I had visits from two arriving astronauts who reported that the sign on the end of 575 was legible from the aircraft approach pattern for a great distance before landing at Patrick.

Within a little over an hour I had an irate Air Force Lt. Col from the Air Installations Office shouting at me that the sign was unauthorized and should be promptly removed from the building. I told him that I felt that General Yates' approval was really enough to leave it there. He said that he was sure General Yates would not approve. I told him that I was sure that he had indicated pleasure at its appearance that morning. He said flatly, "I don't believe that." I reached for the phone and said, "Lets ask him." He turned a little pale. I dialed Capt. Hap Woldt's number (General Yates aide) and when the secretary connected him I said, "Hap, wasn't General Yates pleased with our new NASA sign when he saw it this morning?" At the other end of the line there was a momentary silence, then Hap said, "Mr. Byrnes I don't know what in hell you're talking about." I said "That's what I thought too, Hap. Thanks a lot" and hung up. I sort of shrugged at the unhappy Colonel and he muttered something like "go to hell you, you civilian" and charged out of my office.

As a matter of fact, General Yates did like the sign. But I'm sure that Installations Office never bothered to question him about it.

Part IV
Wanted A New Home: Space Lab

A fast-moving NASA Headquarters decision to mount a Site Selection effort had brought Mr. John Parsons of Ames Research Center, Mr. Philip Miller of Goddard Research Center, Mr. Ed Campagna (Construction Engineer) of Space Task Group, and Mr. Wesley Hjornevik (my boss in Space Task Group Administration) together at Mr. Webb's office for the first step in Site Selection, the Establishment of Criteria. Dr. Robert R. Gilruth and his staff supplied the content of these criteria. Grouped to reflect their weight and importance, they were as follows:

Essential Criteria

-Transportation
Capability to transport by barge, large, cumbersome space vehicles (30 to 40 feet in diameter) to and from water shipping. Preferably the site should have its own or have access to suitable docking facilities. Time required in transport will be considered.

Availability of a first-class, all-weather commercial jet service airport and a Department of Defense air base installation in the general area capable of handling a high-performance military aircraft.

- Communications
Reasonable proximity to main routes of the long-line telephone system.

- Local Industrial Support Labor Supply
An existing, well-established industrial complex, including machine and fabrication shops, to support a research and development activity of high scientific and technical content, and capable of fabricating pilot models of large spacecraft.

A well-established supply of construction contractors and building trades and craftsmen to permit rapid construction of facilities without premium labor costs.

- Community Facilities
Close proximity to a culturally attractive community to permit the recruitment and retention of a staff with a high percentage of professional scientific personnel.

Close proximity to a well-established institution of higher education with emphasis on an institution specializing in the basic sciences and in space-related graduate and postgraduate education and research.

- Electrical Power

Strong local utility system capable of developing up to 80,000 KVA of reliable power.

- Water

Readily available, good quality water capable of supplying 300,000 gallons per day potable and 300,000 gallons per day industrial.

- Area

1,000 usable acres with a suitable adjacent area for further development. Suitable areas in the general location for low hazard and nuisance subsidiary installations requiring some isolation.

- Climate

A mild climate permitting year-round, ice free water transportation; and permitting out-of-door work for most of the year to facilitate operations, reduce facility costs, and speed construction.

Desirable Criteria

- Impact on Area

Compatibility of proposed laboratory with the regional planning that may exist and ability of community facilities to absorb the increased population, and to provide the related industrial and transport support required.

- Site Development Costs

Consideration of cost for site development required for the proposed laboratory.

- Operating Costs

Consideration of costs for normal operations including utility rates, construction costs, wage scales, etc.

- Interim Facilities

Availability of reasonably adequate facilities for the temporary use of up to 1,500 people in the same general areas as the permanent site.

On the afternoon of August 16, 1961, I received word that Mr. Hjornevik was ill with a kidney infection at his home and that his doctor would not agree to his participation in the Site Survey trip which was about to begin. I was to contact Dr. Gilruth and arrange for my appointment as an alternate for Wes. This I did and a wire went out to Dr. Silverstein requesting the change. I joined the group in Washington the next day.

They were in the process of screening several hundred locations proposals from all over the country. It was agreed that, of the primary criteria, the one on weather might best serve as a start at applying our measuring rod to this mass of proposals. It was eventually decided that the requirement for an all-year-round outdoor climate really referred to cold weather, partly for outdoor testing and center construction and certainly in relations to the anticipated need for barging capability. Therefore, we asked the U.S. Weather Bureau to draw us an isotherm for a 32° low mean temperature for the coldest month of the year.

The result was quite interesting. The area outlined included all of the old hometown favorites

Moon Child: Growing Up NASA

of the Space Task Group family; Langley for some; Florida and the Gulf Coast for others; and the West Coast for us old Desert Rats and California devotees. On the map the isotherm ran south along the East Coast starting just above the mouth of the Chesapeake Bay across southern Georgia and Alabama along the Gulf Coast. It passed south into Mexico near the Great Divide and emerged again in Arizona and went up the West Coast nearly to Seattle before it curved out to sea.

The Site proposals above this line we agreed to eliminate from consideration unless some overwhelming reason developed indicating that a particular one should be reconsidered.

In screening the advance material provided along with proposals of sites (in some cases these were very detailed presentations), we applied the rest of the prime criteria to the remaining locations as well as a dozen or so possible locations suggested to be considered as logical sites by the Site Survey Team members.

On the afternoon of _____, the four of us met with Dr. Abe Silverstein to report what we were prepared to propose to Mr. Webb as an inspection itinerary. The trip would include Jacksonville, Tampa, Baton Rouge, Houston, San Diego and A___ (although a site inspection trip to Alaska took place by my father I believe this to be Atlanta).

Abe suggested that we limit our attention to the lower east coast, the Gulf coast and California.

A meeting had also been scheduled immediately with Mr. James Webb and Dr. Hugh Dryden. The Survey Team with Dr. Silverstein took a cab from the office of Manned Space Flight at 19th and H to the old Cosmos Club building (1420 H Street, N.E.)

across Lafayette Park cata-cornered from the White House where Mr. Webb's Headquarters flag flew.

I remember that during the ride along H Street, we kidded Abe about the old days at Lewis Lab, Cleveland, and that he made a comment that he was thinking about chucking the whole Washington rat race and asking for the Director's job back at Lewis Lab which was still vacant since Dr. Raymond Sharpe's death months before; obviously, now, I recognize this remark as a foreshadow of his return to Cleveland and the appointment of Mr. Brainerd Holmes as the nation's boss of Manned Space Flight.

Site Survey plans were, of course, the main topic during the ride; and when we arrived at Mr. Webb's office, his secretary, and Miss Jo Debilla, Dr. Dryden's secretary, were both calmly handling a frenzy of jingling telephones. The receiver-end scraps that you can't help hearing, and in this case find it impossible to forget, went something like this. As Dr. Dryden appeared at his office door and told us to come in, we said hello to Franklin Phillips, Special Assistant to Mr. Webb and long-time acquaintance from NACA days.

The telephone traffic went on a pace... "Yes Sir, I know that Senator Kerr is waiting; Mr. Webb will be off long distance any moment now, thank you for being patient"... "Yes Sir, he's here, but he's on long distance. Could Mr. Phillips help you?"... "All Right, sir, I'll tell him and I'm sure he'll call you right back. Thank you, sir."... "Administrator's Office"... "Well, he just finished one long distance call and started another. May I have him call the Congressman as soon as he can? Oh, I'm sure it will only be a half-hour or so. Thank you, Alice -- things are really humming over here today"... "Administrators Office"...

We were joined in Dr. Dryden's office by Abe Hyatt, Ralph Ulmer, and Paul Dembling. Dr. Dryden and Dr. Silverstein talked about current budget problems and a management detail or two. Then the Administrator, Jim Webb, a picture of energy and eagerness in the midst of the tumult of attention which we knew he was weathering at the moment, strode into Dr. Dryden's office and we were introduced all around. Mr. Parsons outlined our proposal of the sites which we would inspect and our approach to evaluating them. I am sure from later comments by the rest of the survey team that we were all affected by Mr. Webb's tremendous drive and enthusiasm, "vigor" if you will. He instructed us that (1) it had been intended that our survey would be a silent, unheralded passage through the tour, but that (2) pressures from Congressional and local officials had made it clear that wherever we went NASA Headquarters, Mr. Dembling's Congressional Affairs Office, would have to keep the District Congressman and the Senators from the state advised in advance of our complete itinerary, (3) we were not to worry about this political activity, but we were to let the NASA Headquarters people, Mr. Webb's office, Mr. Dembling and Mr. Ulmer, handle that part of the job, (4) we were to make an objective report on each site we inspected in the light of the established criteria, (5) we were to submit our objective evaluation to Mr. Webb on our return without a recommendation.

Mr. Webb made a careful final review of these points and re-emphasized that in the end the responsibility for deciding this "hot potato" was his and he expected to take full responsibility for it. The implication was in his comments, as I recall quite vividly, that the White House had made this clear to him; and he was making it doubly clear to us. The meeting ended with the usual "good luck and let us know if you need anything... Keep in touch." ... and off we went.

We really went home to explain to our wives that we were going off to see the world below the 32° isotherm.

On Sunday night we assembled with a special assist from the Jacksonville Chamber of Commerce, at our first Florida stop at the Hotel.

Selecting a site for the Manned Spacecraft Center was, to say the least, a lively experience. The location of the new facility drew a gigantic amount of attention, and the field survey trip alone at times assumed an air of the old three-ring circus coming to town.

As I have said, the original plans to move the Space Task Group to Goddard Space Center at Greenbelt, Maryland had been discarded. The requirements for building an entirely new center had already been given considerable attention. What your mission is and what you have to use to carry it out (what buildings, what facilities, what support industry) have vital bearing, of course, on where you want to locate.

About this time our big concern over the problem of where in the U.S. would we put this new "Manned Spacecraft Development Center" had hit home with people at NASA Headquarters in Washington. About the same time, also, it was becoming an interesting item to home-loyal congressmen and local politicians all over the country.

Alan Shepard's first Mercury venture into space brought a tremendous concentration of attention to the program. First, the Presidential telephone call to Al aboard the USS Lake Champlain at sea; then the big parade-type return to the U.S.; then Alan's masterful handling of his report to the special joint reception to Congress; and the international approbation of the U.S. Space effort all took place in rapid succession and suddenly the all-out U.S. Space program was really launched.

On May 25, 1961 President Kennedy went to the Congress with a special message on urgent national needs. Part of this message dealt with Defense requirements, economic and social problems at home and abroad, disarmament and, principally, it was an official position on the "Space Race".

President Kennedy said:

"These are extraordinary times. And we face an extraordinary challenge. Our strength as well as our convictions have imposed upon this nation the role of leader in freedom's cause.

"No role in history could be more difficult or more important. We stand for freedom. That is our conviction for ourselves -- that is our only commitment to others. No friend, no neutral and no adversary should think otherwise. We are not against any man -- or any nation -- or any system -- except as it is hostile to freedom. Nor am I here to present a new military doctrine, bearing any one name or aimed at any one area. I am here to promote the freedom doctrine.

"Finally, if we are to win the battle that is now going on around the world between freedom and tyranny, the dramatic achievements in space which occurred in recent weeks should have made clear to us all, as did the Sputnik in 1957, the impact of this adventure on the minds of men everywhere, who are attempting to make a determination of which road they should take. Since early in my term, our efforts in space have been under review. With the advice of the Vice President, who is Chairman of the National Space Council, we have examined where we are strong and where we are not, where we may succeed and where we may not. Now it is time to take longer strides -- time for a great new American enterprise -- time for this nation to take a clearly leading role in space achievement, which in many ways may hold the key to our future on earth.

"I believe we possess all the resources and talents necessary. But the facts of the matter are that we have never made the national decisions or marshaled the national resources required for such leadership. We have never specified long-range goals on an urgent time schedule, or managed our resources and our time so as to insure their fulfillment.

"Recognizing the head start obtained by the Soviets with their large rocket engines, which gives them many months of lead-time, and recognizing the likelihood that they will exploit this lead for some time to come in still more impressive successes, we nevertheless are required to make new efforts on our own. For a while we cannot guarantee that we shall one day be first, we can guarantee that any failure to make this effort will make us last. We take an additional risk by making it in full view of the world -- but as shown by the feat of astronaut Shepard, this very risk enhances our stature when we are successful. But this is not merely a race. Space is open to us now; and our eagerness to share its meaning is not governed by the efforts of others. We go into space because whatever mankind must undertake, free men must fully share.

"I therefore ask the Congress, above and beyond the increases I have earlier requested for space activities, to provide the funds which are needed to meet the following national goals:

"First, I believe that this nation should commit itself to achieving the goal, before this decade is out, of landing a man on the moon and returning him safely to the earth. No single space project in this period will be more impressive to mankind, or more important for the long-range exploration of space; and none will be so difficult or expensive to accomplish. We propose to accelerate development of the appropriate lunar space craft. We propose to develop alternate liquid and solid fuel boosters, much larger than any now being developed, until certain which is superior. We propose additional funds for other engine development and for unmanned explorations -- explorations which are particularly important for one purpose which this nation will never overlook: the survival of the man who first makes this daring flight. But in a very real sense, it will not be one man going to the moon -- and if we make this judgment affirmatively, it will be an entire nation. For all of us must work to put him there.

"Secondly, and additional 23 million dollars, together with 7 million dollars already available, to accelerate development of the ROVER nuclear rocket. This gives promise of some day providing a means for even more exiting and ambitious exploration of space, perhaps beyond the moon, perhaps to the very end of the solar system itself.

"Third, an additional 50 million dollars will make the most of our present leadership, by accelerating the use of space satellites for the world-wide communications.

"Fourth, an additional 75 million dollars -- of which 53 million dollars is for the Weather Bureau -- will help give us at the earliest possible time a satellite system for world-wide weather observation.

"Let's be clear -- and this is a judgment which the Members of Congress must finally make -- let it be clear that I am asking the Congress and the country to accept a firm commitment to a new course of action -- a course which will last for many years and carry very heavy costs of 531 million dollars in fiscal 1962 -- and estimated seven to nine billion dollars additional over the next five years. If we are to go only half way, or reduce our sights in the face of difficulty, in my judgment it would be better not to go at all.

"Now this is a choice which this country must make, and I am confident that under the leadership of the Space Committees of the Congress, and the Appropriating Committees, that you will consider the matter carefully.

"It is a most important decision that we make as a nation. But all of you have lived through the last four years and have seen the significance of space and the adventures in space, and no one can predict with certainty what the ultimate meaning will be of mastery of space.

"I believe we should go to the moon. But I think every citizen of this country as well as the Member of the Congress should consider the matter carefully in making their judgment, to which we have given attention over many weeks and months, because it is a heavy burden, and there is no sense in agreeing or desiring that the United States take an affirmative position in outer space, unless we are prepared to do the work and bear the burdens to make it successful. If we are not, we should decide today and this year.

"This decision demands a major national commitment of scientific and technical manpower, material and facilities, and the possibility of their diversion from other important activities where they are already thinly spread. It means a degree of dedication, organization and discipline which have not always characterized our research and development efforts. It means we cannot afford undue work stoppages, inflated costs of material or talent, wasteful inter-agency rivalry, or high turnover of key personnel.

"New objectives and new money cannot solve these problems. They could in fact, aggravate them further -- unless every scientist, every engineer, every serviceman, every technician, contractor, and civil servant gives his personal pledge that this nation will move forward, with the full speed of freedom, in the exciting adventure of space."

Moving words from a leader capable of inspiring action in everyone with imagination enough to picture the great new era just opening to mankind. The envelope within which man's thoughts, his plans, his aspirations had been cast was now opened to infinity and we could see within our lifetime the possibility of men visiting and exploring at least the earth's nearby neighbors in the universe.

The challenge of the task and the spell of our success and the leadership of the President carried the field and Congress approved the U.S. Space Program as proposed by NASA.

MSC RELOCATION REPORT

We realized early that the essential element necessary to get an aggressive national effort for manned space exploration on the road was the capability to manage the development of large manned space-craft and to operate the spacecraft as well as the related ground support systems. This portion of the total job was in itself one of the largest, if not the largest, research and development job ever undertaken by man in war or peace.

As it stood in 1960 the nation was committed to the fact that the Space Task Group had been successfully handling the Mercury program using a full range of industry and Government resources. However, a space program of a much larger magnitude would require a great expansion of staff and facilities, and the institution of organization and management concepts consistent with the new role of the Space Task Group. How, and how effectively this capability was to be generated would have a direct bearing on the success or failure of the total program.

We made several basic assumptions as a basis for the organization and management approach which we used.

These were:

1. There would be an independent NASA field center responsible for the conduct of programs for Manned spacecraft.

2. In the conduct of such programs, primary reliance would be placed on industrial contractors for detailed design and fabrication of the spacecraft and associated systems and subsystems.

3. Basic research support would be provided by other Government and private organizations.

4. The maintenance and operation of worldwide tracking and data acquisition stations would be the responsibility of the NASA Goddard Space Flight Center and other Government agencies. (This was based on a NASA Headquarter's decision already in effect at that time.)

5. That vehicle (booster) development would be the responsibility of Marshall Space Flight Center. (Vehicle-spacecraft integration would be a mutual responsibility between our Center and Marshall.)

These assumptions provided us with a broad outline of the basic parameters within which the organization and management proposals were developed for our Director, Dr. Bob Gilruth, to present to the Administrator, Mr. Webb in Washington. The proposed plan took an approach which we felt was designed to provide the greatest possible flexibility and efficiency in the use of leadership manpower.

This plan provided for the following:

1. The Center would be organized so that multiple programs relating to the manned space flight could be coordinated and conducted simultaneously.

2. The internal organization of the Center must be established to provide for the detailed direction of each of these projects at a level below that of the Center Director.

3. The Center would be responsible for the conception of new missions and projects.

4. The Director must be provided sufficient tools for independent evaluation of on-going programs and projects.

5. The Center must be in a position to respond to the higher echelon requirements for project information and reports.

6. The Center would maintain "in-house" necessary skills to:
    a. perform mission conception and preliminary design studies

    b. prepare specifications

    c. evaluate detailed specifications

    d. monitor the work of the contractor

    e. assure proper systems and subsystems integration

    f. perform necessary test and check-out functions

    g. operate the systems and spacecraft required by the programs

7. The Center would be supported by its own technical services (design and shop support and administrative support).

8. The Center would have a competence in the space medicine field to handle life support systems and crew equipment development surveillance.

The organization which we proposed is shown on the attached chart (not included at time of this book's publication). As will be noted, this plan proposed in part the establishment of a Project Manager's office for each Project assigned to the Center or expected to be assigned to it. Because of the close inter-relationship between the several projects, a Development Projects Manager was suggested to coordinate the work of the Project Managers and maintain a balance between them. In addition, a number of directors were proposed to be responsible for flight systems, test and evaluation, life systems, flight operations, data systems and computation. The relationship which would be established between the Project Managers and these "functional directors" would be that commonly found in most project management organizations. This portion of the plan was changed considerably prior to the first approval of the Center's organization in that the "Development Projects manager" was never created and the Project Mangers reported to the Director without the intermediate step.

Under this concept, the Project Manager's position as we proposed it, was to be basically a man responsible for the following functions:

1. Over-all planning of the project activities including determination of resource requirements.

2. Placing "job orders" on the functional directors for necessary project work. (These directors would be then responsible for the actual engineering design or tests required.)

3. Coordinating and integrating the work performed by the functional directors for the project, including making determinations as to approach.

4. Developing design specifications (in conjunction with the functional directors) and approving detailed specifications.

5. Serving as Chairman of the Source Selection Boards required.

6. Monitoring contractor operations (relying on support form the functional directors as required).

7. Arranging with the Director of Test and Evaluation for conduct of necessary tests of subsystems and systems.

8. Approving modifications in design as proposed by the contractor or resulting from test results.

9. Developing flight operational plans (in conjunction with the flight operations groups and the training group.)

10. Coordinating flight operations.

11. Performing all necessary related management functions including developing resource information for budgetary planning, reporting on the status of schedules as required by higher echelons, and similar matters.

Of primary importance in this plan for Project Management were the following considerations:

1. The Project Manager would not supervise the functional Directors.

2. Functional Directors would be responsible for providing support to the Project Manager -- on assignment -- on the basis of predetermined "levels of effort".

3. Requirements which the Project Manager developed and which exceeded predetermined "levels of effort" would require the approval of the Central Director.

4. The Project Manager would be completely responsible through the Development Projects.

5. Manager to the Center Director for all phases of project work.

6. The Project Manager would rely on the Assistant Director for Administration for the provision of necessary administrative support services.

Under this plan of organization also, certain staff resources would have to be established reporting directly to the Center Director. These would include: an Office of Mission Analysis and Evaluation responsible for conducting studies of advanced missions; and Office of Reliability and Flight Safety; and an Office of Program Schedules and Reports.

In our memorandum recommending the Center's adoption of this plan for presentation to NASA Headquarters, we argued that it provided the following advantages important to any project management system:

1. This plan of organization fixes responsibility for all project activities in a single individual -- the Project Manager.

2. This plan provides a mechanism -- short of the Director and Associate Director -- for coordination of project activities.

3. This plan provides for the development of strong, centralized, functional divisions providing support for all projects. Scarce skills are conserved and maximum utilization of staff results from combining all personnel doing similar support work into single functional divisions.

4. The Central Director is freed from the day-to-day problems associated with any single project. He is able to concentrate his efforts

on over-all Center direction. Center-Headquarters and inter-agency relationships, and advanced mission planning.

5. This plan provides for a centralized and effective administrative and technical services support organization to "back up" Center technical operations.

6. This plan provides the Center Director with an independent Mission Analysis and Evaluation Group to perform studies in the conception of new missions and to evaluate on-going Center projects.

7. The plan of organization is traditional and, therefore, can be better understood by those outside the Center.

A development center with these capabilities must have the facilities for effective operation. This would be true even though the Center were basically an engineering management activity concerned with organizing basically an engineering management activity concerned with organizing and supervising the work of industrial contractors, industry, universities and government support. In addition to office space, the facilities required would be of three basic types: (1) a large national facility for the environmental testing of large spacecraft; (2) an equipment evaluation laboratory for the support of all program participants; and (3) large scale mission simulators and trainers for flight crews and ground crews as well as certain types of tests.

These facilities and the required manpower as our management, our scientists, and our construction people saw them in this hasty "first cut" analysis of what the big new Center needed were:

Facility	No. Housed	Estimated Cost
Managed Space Flight Project Facility	1,315	$12,133,000
Equipment Evaluation Laboratory & Support Facility	910	13,245,000
Flight Operations Facility	280	3,600,000
Environment Test Laboratory	165	26,310,000
	2,670	$55,288,000
Cost of Utilities and Site Development		4,540,000
Total		$59,828,000

Now most of this estimating was done "in a vacuum" without more than a hurried set of verbal instructions from NASA Headquarters and utilization of earlier facilities planning done by the Goddard Center during the formative period when we had been expected to move to the Greenbelt to join them.

The basic group of personnel around which this Center must be built was the 500 man Space Task Group, temporarily housed in space in the old east area of the Langley Research Center at Langley Air Force Base in Virginia. These facilities were badly crowded and there were no further adequate buildings in which we could expand. No land was available in the east area of Langley Field for new construction; some land might have been obtained in the west area of Langley Field where the main facilities of the Langley Research Center were located.

The big question on everyone's mind in the Space Task Group in those days of mid-1961 aside from preoccupation with Mercury's engineering facts-of-life difficulties was, "Where will we move?" For a few of the roughly 500, maybe 70 or so, it was more like, "Will we really have to move?"

A high pressure effort was mounted by the Langley Research Center officials aimed at convincing NASA Headquarters people that this activity should remain right where it was. These folks of Langley, the old NACA grandmother center of them all, sought to retain proximity to what they saw as a massive newborn Space giant in the hope of (1) absorbing and controlling it, or (2) drawing new monetary strength from it.

In the summer of 1960 Walt Williams had asked me to run a quick study of the why's and wherefore's of getting the show on the road for a move to Goddard, to the Cape, to anywhere. The quarters were becoming cramped in the old 1930 NACA Langley buildings and we were doing things to create new space, like looking at the old seaplane hangar and the Langley Yacht Club as our next move.

This quick study of the situation showed that about 30 percent of the land area in the Peninsula district of Virginia (Hampton, Warwick, and Yorktown) was being utilized by the U.S. Government and over 60 per cent of the Peninsula's income was directly dependent upon the Government's activities there. In anybody's book, this was of course an unhealthy situation economically.

A general examination of the relationship of the STG to the NASA field structure was conducted in fall in the 1960. A number of alternative solutions to Center location were examined.

It was the STG Management's view then, and I am sure remains, that the greatest total advantage to NASA and the taxpayer, both in terms of the manned space flight effort and the advanced research program, would be in the establishment of a new Center at a new location rather than at Langley or any existing facility. The most compelling reasons for this belief were:

    1. The increased pace and scope of the space effort would require a total increase in resources of the agency including its basic and applied research. The location of a development center at Langley would tend

to warp this basic Research Center in the direction of the immediate hardware problems.

2. The program of manned space flight and operation laid out for the future meant that the new Center must be in a position to draw heavily on the nations total resources. Thus, Langley and other NSA internal support, while significant at that point in 1961, would be proportionately less in the future.

3. NASA was already heavily concentrated in the areas where the existing Centers were located and a new location could be selected which would strengthen our ability to tap the resources of a new area of the country.

4. The present transitional character of the manned space flight program indicated that a well managed move could result in a minimal disruption of the program.

In September and October of 1960, a NASA Headquarters group studied the problem of location of the Space Task Group and a Life Sciences Field Center which was then proposed. At that time the Space Task Group was a part of Goddard Space Flight Center as has been said, and was slated for physical union with the other elements of Goddard at Beltsville, Maryland location.

The guidelines given the study group restricted consideration to three sites -- NASA Centers: Goddard in Maryland, Langley in Virginia or Ames in California. Its considerations related to the advantages of each of these sites in terms of the availability of support for the manned space effort, the impact on the research program of NASA, the pertinence of the close geographical proximity between Life Sciences and Space Task Group and possible organizational arrangements at each site. The group was not asked to make recommendations but rather to pull together the considerations and view of the NASA people involved.

Here is a summary of the findings of this study group:

1. Manned Space Flight would assume a very large importance in NASA's program and should be based on a field arm of center size and status.

2. Langley's principal advantages lie in the fact that the location of the Space Task Group was at that site and the larger and broader scientific and facility support it could provide to manned space activity.

3. Goddard as a location had little to commend it.

4. The primary advantages of Ames were adjacency to the NASA Life Sciences Field Center and a lesser impact on NSA's research capability.

5. Organizationally, two strong sets of views were found:
    a. Those who consider a separation of research and development necessary for the preservation of research strongly favored a single, integrated center.

Moon Child: Growing Up NASA

    b. Those who believe close and responsible association of applied research with advanced development necessary to the meaningfulness and quality of the research strongly favored a single, integrated center.

A third opposed the integrated center on the grounds of a NASA need for increased capability and advocated a co-located center as an addition to present capabilities in view of the magnitude to NASA's total job.

6. A move of the Space Task Group is not feasible until the fall of 1961 at the earliest.

Based on NASA's Ten Year Plan as it appeared in 1961, it was clear as I have said before, that the contemplated effort would be one of the biggest and most complex research and development programs ever undertaken. Its accomplishment, even assuming maximum utilization of the Nation's industrial capabilities, would require a major, highly competent technical and managerial organization.

Three possibilities for the permanent location of the Space Task Group deserve serious consideration:

1. A separate center co-located with the Langley Research Center at Langley Field, Virginia.

2. An integrated research and hardware development center at Langley.

3. A completely new site.

Ames was eliminated in view of the already heavy Government concentration of activities, both in-house and contract, on the West Coast.

Co-located Center at Langley

Under this concept the Space Task Group would be organized as a largely independent entity located on land owned by NASA at Langley Field. Two center management structures would exist side by side reporting to different points in NSA Headquarters. One of the centers (presumably the older Langley Research Center) would represent NASA to the community and common services (large shops, building and ground maintenance, physical security, etc.) for both centers.

The three basic premises behind this proposal were: (1) a complete organizational separation must be maintained between a hardware development activity and a research activity in order to prevent serious diversion of the research effort into the high pressure hardware development program; (2) a move to a new site with the attendant drain on resources for planning and the temporary disruption of the activity involved in a geographical move should be avoided; and (3) major scientific, technical and facility support (estimated at about 50 per cent of all support) was coming to STG at that time from the Langley Research Center. It would be advantageous to continue to have such support immediately adjacent.

Major Pros and Cons
Pros
1. Maximum assurance of program continuity without disruption.

2. Less deleterious impact on the research effort than the integrated center alternate.

3. High proportion of scientific, technical and facility support immediately adjacent.

Integrated Center at Langley

This alternative visualized an integrated center at Langley with manned space flight as its major mission. It would contemplate a single administrative and technical service organization. The technical organization would have two major components: (1) development project management, and (2) research. A major premise would be that the research effort could be adequately protected in field by the director of such a center. Some economy in people could result from a single administrative structure, but a total center strength of about 5,500 would be required. Facility requirements would be the same as in the co-located alternative.

The pros and cons for this alternate were essentially the same as for co-located alternate with the following major exceptions:

1. This alternate on its face had an aura of permanence and significance to it. It could be publicly dramatized as a major step in the development of manned space flight.

2. Would create a NASA field structure, highlighted by two major centers with the two major assignments, i.e., boosters and manned spacecraft.

3. Would be more economical than co-located centers and more acceptable to those outside NASA (Bureau of the Budget, Congress, etc.).

A Completely New Site

The third alternative is to establish a manned space flight center at a new site building with the present Space Task Group Staff. This would be a complete break with the Langley environment and geographically separate center from one of its major sources of support. Functional concepts, operating methods and management philosophy would not change. However, a new self-sufficient center would require facilities and staffing somewhat greater than that required under the first two alternative.

Pros and Cons
Pros
1. Could extend to a new section of the country an opportunity to contribute to the space effort and give a better geographical distribution to NASA field activities.

2. Could increase NASA's total capability without any sacrifice of existing research capability.

3. Could afford an opportunity for a close tie with a new group of local colleges and universities.

Cons
1. Could present a problem of temporary program dislocation in making the move. It would necessitate a major relocation of staff and their families and undoubtedly short

term effects on efficiency. It should be noted, however, that many of the Space Task Group staff were "camping" until a firm decision on location would be made. This fact could, in some degree, minimize the trauma involved in a move.

2. Could entail, somewhat, costs in facilities and personnel.

3. Could geographically separate the group from its major current source of scientific and facility support.

4. Could precipitate a time-consuming tug-of-war over site selection.

Manned Space Flight Laboratory Location

James E. Webb, Administer of NASA, announced September 19, 1961 completion of the study to determine the location of the agency's new $60,000,000 Manned Space Flight Laboratory. The facility was authorized by Congress for initiation in the current Fiscal year. The laboratory will be located in Houston, Texas on 1,000 acres of land to be made available to the government by Rice University. The land, in Harris County, borders on Clear Lake and on the Houston Light and Power Company Salt Water Canal.

The Manned Space Flight Laboratory will be the command center for the Manned Lunar Landing mission and all the follow-on manned space flight missions. It will be utilized to design, develop, evaluate and test the spacecraft for Project Apollo as well as all of its subsystems and to train the crew that will fly these missions. The FY 62 appropriation provided funds for the development of a site, and construction of 4 integrated facilities: (1) a flight project facility, (2) an equipment evaluation laboratory, (3) a flight operations facility and (4) an environmental testing lab.

Mr. Webb pointed out that the recently announced expansion of the Atlantic Missile Range at Cape Canaveral, Florida, as the launch site for the very large space vehicle to be constructed, and with the establishment of a fabrication facility at the Michoud plant near the mouth of the Mississippi River at New Orleans, the location of the new laboratory at Houston would facilitate the establishment of an integrated facilities system connected by deep water transportation and capable of handling the large space craft and launch vehicles in the Apollo manned lunar landing projects.

This grouping of the facilities in a region permitting out-of-door work for most of the year provides flexibility and a capability of expansion to meet the needs of a very large vehicle which present projections indicate will be required for heavier payloads and deeper penetration into space beyond the moon to the planets.

In Late April 1961 I was in Washington working temporarily at NASA Headquarters on a budget presentation on the requirements of setting up a Manned Spacecraft Center when Walt Williams called me from the Cape. He asked, "What are you doing now?" I explained. He said, "O.K. get back to Langley and get your seagoing clothes, you are going out on the carrier Champlain. Be here tomorrow morning. The Mission Review is at 9 o'clock." The next day I arrived at the Cape and went to Engineering and Operations building in the Hangar "S" area. The Mission Review, one of the final steps before launch, was taking place. I came in late and sat in the back and my boss spotted me in the crowd.

All of the major components of the mission, the booster, the spacecraft, the recovery forces, the Weather Bureau, etc. made their reports. They completed their general reports on systems status and everything seemed satisfactory. Then Walt said, "Well, now as a result of a session we had yesterday where some of the NASA components of the operation were in disagreement, I am going to designate a head man for NASA for the seagoing operation of the recovery forces. All NASA people aboard the Naval vessels of the recovery forces at sea will be under Mr. Marty Byrnes who will act for me. He will be sure that we present a single face to the Navy during the recovery operation." Now this was quite a shock. I had gathered that I was replacing Astronaut Schirra as a liaison man aboard the Champlain but I had been away from the recovery end of the mission activity for quite a while in the process of planning the new Center, and had to get up to speed in sort of a hurry.

Shortly after that the meeting finished and I started looking around for Bob Thompson who was Head of the Space Task Group Recovery Branch. He indicated that there was a Naval aircraft taking off for Mayport in a matter of 45 minutes and if I wanted to go to Mayport I would be aboard. I didn't like this sort of approach so I told him that when the airplane left it better not leave without me. I had to talk to my boss about what we were specifically expected to do. I found Mr. Williams and we talked briefly about what my responsibilities were. Mainly, it was trying the seagoing Aeromed's, the Public Affairs people and Recovery

Technical troops together while we were working with the Navy during Al's mission. The day before, these three groups had been involved in a sturdy set of complaints and counter-complaints about whether the PAO could or would keep the press pool members who were to accompany us, clear of the medical and technical operation enough to avoid interference with the strict astronaut debriefing control and the spacecraft security. A similar problem was also stewing between the Aeromeds and the Technical Recovery people.

After I had obtained this general idea of what the problem was, I sought out Dr. White and Dr. Douglas. Dr. White was of course, the over-all medical chief for Mercury and Dr. Douglas was the astronaut's doctor. I asked what I could do for them in this particular case. Stan White said, "Well, it's obvious why you were picked, you are the diplomate and peacemaker." I asked Dr. Douglas what he thought. He said, "Well, just be sure you don't let the public relations people take any pictures of any dead, dying or bloody astronauts. Then I found Bob Thompson again and said, "Look, what can I do for you, I want to keep this thing all together." He said, "Well, I'm going to Mayport with you and I will take care of technically briefing the Navy on how we are expected to perform here." Then I found Shorty Powers. I said, "Pappy, what's going on, how come your people are in a flap with the other tow sides of the house here?" He said, "Oh I guess it's just that we want as much mileage out of this as we can get. You've got the feel. You understand what I want. Just make sure my boys don't get cut off entirely out there. You're going to have in the neighborhood of a 14-man press pool aboard the carrier with you." I also knew the background of what the STG wanted in the way of privacy for the astronaut during the debriefing period and I knew we had to set up whatever we could in this regard.

The Task Force assigned to recover astronaut Alan Shepard and his MR-3 spacecraft "Freedom 7" was under command of Rear Admiral F.V.H. Hilles, Commander of Destroyer Flotilla FOUR of the Atlantic Fleet and Commander, Project Mercury Recovery Forces.

The task force carrier and destroyers were in port at Mayport near Jacksonville, Florida preparing to put to sea when we went aboard on Friday afternoon, April 28. A group of us were flown to Mayport by the Navy plane which I have mentioned, and were met by special vehicles and taken to the dock area where the ships were moored. Charlie Tynan, Bob Thompson and I were welcomed aboard by Commander H.H. Skidmore and shortly thereafter met Captain Roual Weymough, the carrier skipper, and finally the Admiral.

The Commander of the Task Group, Admiral G. P. Koch, was a salty old gentleman and he had all the air of a real commanding officer. There wasn't any question about that. He invited us to accept assignment to meals in the flag mess and indicated that he wanted to get down to business right away.

We were joined on board at intervals during the afternoon by Dick Mittauer and Al Alibrando of the NASA Public Affairs office who went about making arrangements for briefings for the press pool. The press pool members, each representing areas of the interest among the news media, also arrived at the Champlain by various modes of transportation during the afternoon. Separate from the press pool photographers was Dean Conger of National Geographic, on loan to NASA for special astronaut coverage.

The Aeromedical team of doctors, Commander R. C. Lanning and Army Captain M.J. Strong, arrived as scheduled and set about preparing the designated sick bay areas and briefing medical personnel, as well as checking the medical support kits and setting up detailed plans for their operation. They discovered a few major problems which they set about clearing up, the most serious of which was that recent hepatitis on board two of the destroyers made it impossible to use blood donors from those crews in an emergency. The doctors readily arranged with the local Navy hospital at Mayport to obtain emergency blood to be put aboard the tow destroyers in question.

As I said above, Admiral Koch agreed that we should "get the show on the road" right away. We met with his staff and the NASA group soon after arrival on board. He voiced complete satisfaction and agreement with the assignment of a NASA senior representative on board the USS Lake Champlain.

We scheduled a briefing for Mr. Thompson of the Commanders of all of the ships involved and their staffs at Mayport on the evening of April 28 to set the proper atmosphere to lay detailed on-board plans. An earlier briefing of senior staff members of the force at Cape Canaveral had prepared these few with very useful knowledge of the program. The MR-2 recovery film and the helicopter sling technique film were also useful in this briefing. The ships crews were not very familiar with Project Mercury. We arranged, through material handled by Mittauer, Alibrando, and Tynan, to have films shown on the Lake Champlain and on the destroyers and to disseminate through the ships' news sheets and public address systems a reasonable familiarization course on Mercury. As the mission progressed on board the Champlain, we also kept a sequence of announcements going on the status of the countdown. Out there we really missed the continuous direct contact with what was going on in the Control Center as well as the ever helpful coverage of the commercial TV which even at that early date in the program was always technically accurate and, thanks to Shorty Powers and Roy Neal of NBC and their efforts, almost as close to the pad and the real time situation as the people in the Mercury Control Center. But that's another story.

Back to the Task Group's preparation for sea. The plan for the mission as reviewed by Bob Thompson for the carrier and destroyer officers had been established several months before by NASA Recovery people working with the Navy.

The Task Group to be dispersed along the trajectory track and in the predicted landing areas were under the command of Admiral Koch. The units of this group included Destroyer Sqaudron Twenty under the command of Captain D.E. Willman.

- USS Champlain (CVS-39) commanded by Capt R. Weymonth, USN
   - USS Decatur (DD 936) commanded by Cdr A.W. McLane, USN
   - USS Wadleigh (DD 689) commanded by LCdr D.W. Kiley, USN
   - USS Rooks (DD 804) commanded by Cdr W.H. Pattilo, USN
   - USS The Sullivans (DD 537) commanded by Cdr F.H.S. Hall, USN
   - USS Abbot (DD 629) commanded by Cdr R.H. Norman, USN
   - USS N.K. Perry (DD 629) commanded by Cdr O.A. Roberts, USN

Air support for this group was to be provided by Patrol Squadron FIVE P2V's commanded by Cdr T.H. Casey, Jr., USN, and supplemented with Air Rescue Aircraft. Carrier and shore based helicopters were to be provided from the Marine Air Group Twenty-Six, commanded by Col. P.T. Johnson, USMC.

A group positioned off shore would consist of two minecraft and the USS Recovery (ARS 43) under the command of LCdr R.H. Taylor, USN.

Another group to be located at Cape Canaveral consisted of numerous land vehicles and small craft from the Air Force Missile Test Center and were under the command of Lt. Col. Harry E. Cannon, USAF.

After technically briefing the ship's crews we met with the Admiral and the Champlain's Captain Weymouth to establish rough onboard procedures for the carrier.

Mr. Tynan checked the ships crew members of his recovery team and found that they were not fully familiar with their role in capsule handling. He inspected other preparations on board the Lake Champlain. The Navy crew had built a landing pad for the capsule which was a heavy timber dolly with a deck about 20 x 25 feet in size and which was mounted on swivel casters and padded on top with salvaged mattresses. It was decided that Mr. Tynan should visit the destroyers and assist with their capsule handling preparations while we were still in port.

A press briefing was held on the Champlain in the afternoon on April 29 during which Admiral Koch and the NSA representative introduced the MR-3 teams, the carrier officers, and the destroyer officers, and provided a general project and mission familiarization. Commander Nivens, of Destroyer Flotilla Four, had returned from the Patrick Press Briefing and assisted with this briefing also. Mittauer, Alibrando, and I met with the press pool members and the ships officers and provided more detailed project and mission briefing and the details of the press activities aboard ships, principally aboard the carrier, were worked out. The destroyers put to sea on the night of April 30. We were to follow the next morning on the high tide about 9:00 a.m.

On Sunday, April 30, a series of meetings had covered the main areas of Recovery effort on the carrier. The following procedures were worked out for receiving the astronaut when he arrived on board. There were two alternate methods which would be followed, depending on the condition of the astronaut. My report covering these two approaches read as follows:

METHOD ONE (Astronaut either in helicopter or uninjured and able to egress from capsule on its arrival on Lake Champlain)

1. The capsule was to be landed on the specially prepared platform which would be located on the inboard edge of number 2 elevator. The helicopter was to land between spots 4 and 5 marked on the carrier deck.

2. If the astronaut was in the helicopter, he was to be escorted by the NASA doctors to the port catwalk via the ladder just forward of number 2 elevator. He was to proceed via this catwalk to the Flag Mess and then into the Admiral's in-port cabin.

3. If the astronaut was still inside the capsule, but uninjured, he was to leave the capsule and proceed via the route given in (2) above to the Admiral's in-port cabin.

4. Only Mr. Mittauer, NASA PIO, and Captain Eggeman, of the Admiral's Staff were to be allowed in the Flag Mess. The two doctors were to be the only ones allowed with the astronaut in the Admiral's cabin. Two Marines, Hospital Corpsmen, and two photographers (Mr. Conger and one Navy Motor Picture Photographer) were to be in the passageway outside the Flag Mess by the Flag Mess pantry. One of the corpsmen was to be used to take necessary specimen to Sick Bay. He would be accompanied by a Marine to assure his prompt arrival. The photographers were to be on call as directed by the doctors.

METHOD TWO (Astronaut injured)

1. As soon as possible, either before or after the helicopter picked up the capsule, Flag Plot was to be notified via radio that this condition existed. The area around number 3 elevator was to be cleared of all personnel, and the capsule would be landed on the platform which was to be located on number 3 elevator. Number 3 elevator would be lowered into the hangar deck and the special team headed by Mr. Tynan, of NASA Recovery, would remove the astronaut and he would be taken under direction of the Aero-medical team to Sick Bay. The following restrictions on the movement of personnel would be enforced:

2. All press and other personnel would be on the flight deck aft of number 1 barrier. No one would be allowed forward of number 1 barrier on the flight deck, including catwalks, except for those specially cleared and wearing special badges. (The Marine guards, Mr. Tynan's team and the Aeromed team).

3. Press personnel would also be allowed on the 0-5 level (1st level above the deck) of the island and above.

4. The fire doors would be used to isolate hangar bay 2 from hangar bay 1 and no personnel would be allowed on the hangar deck of hangar bay 2 and 3 except for those specially cleared personnel with badges.

5. The ship furnished Marine guards to see that the above plans were followed.

Prior to leaving Mayport, in discussions with the Admirals Staff Communications Officer and the Lake Champlain Communications Officer, we developed a plan based on their previous frequency arrangements and the special news media requirements of which we were aware as a result of the USS Donner experience on earlier launchings. It developed that the Navy was providing, in addition to their operational communications, a three channel teletype news support net. Over this net the Navy communications people had prepared the capacity to transmit to Patrick Air Force Base nearly as fast as the Press Pool could generate copy. It was established that Press transmissions from destroyers of the Task Group would be relayed through the Lake Champlain to the beach.

Working with the ships crew under Cmdr. Skidmore, Mittauer was able to provide the Press Pool with a Press Room immediately adjacent to the ship's Communications Center. This press room was a compartment approximately 15 x 40 feet with desks along both sides. Six typewriters were provided by the Navy. The room had two bulletin boards, a table for Navy biographical and ship's history releases as well as NASA release material, and there was a coffee mess set up at one end "for the use of all personnel." During the countdown the Navy also provided an almost continuous supply of sandwiches and pastry. Copy generated by pool members was submitted to Mr. Alibrando, or to Mr. Mittauer, whoever was on duty. One of these two was to be available at the press room whenever Pool members were there. The ship provided runners to take transmissions to the communication center. A Navy charge-of-quarters manned the press room around the clock during countdown. The Navy communications dispatcher was instructed to transmit releases in the priority order assigned by NASA. Navy personnel operated three tape-punching machines in order to provide rapid handling of copy during the countdown and especially after recovery. As releases were transmitted to the beach, a copy of the outgoing message was brought to the Press Room where it was initialed by the author and placed on a clipboard for general review.

Photographic coverage for NASA was handled by Conger and a team of Navy still and motion picture photographers. News media photographers were not happy with the restrictions which we had to impose upon them. They worked from the first and second levels of the island above the flight deck or from behind barrier number 1 on the flight deck. The Navy was most cooperative in arranging for COD lifts to the beach for news media film, both during the delay between countdowns and after recovery, in sending a film bearing aircraft to Patrick shortly after the departure of the astronaut for G.B.I.

During the countdown it was evident that the Navy crew on board both the destroyers and aboard the carrier, were most anxious to know what was going on back on the beach. And suddenly I discovered that I was about the only man aboard, outside of Chuck Tynan, who really knew what should be happening back there during the countdown. Our communications were not nearly as good as I had expected they would be. As a matter of fact we dug up a copy of a countdown timeline sheet which had been previously released through the press. We did a little bit of dressing up on this and made it show minute by minute what the astronaut would be doing from midnight through the scheduled launch time. We published this count on the various bulletin boards on the ships. This of course, gave the crew a little bit more of a sense of participating.

One of the things that Admiral Koch asked, was whether he should roll out the whole force at 3:00 a.m. to get them ready for launch time which was at 7:00 o'clock. My feeling was that this was kind of ridiculous because we never in the past, even unmanned, had met an exact launch time. There had been in each previous countdown several holds which moved launch up to 8:00 or 9:00 o'clock. So it seemed pretty silly to awaken and alert everybody on board at 3:00 o'clock in the morning to wait for something that wasn't going to happen until many hours later.

During the course of the countdown, one of the things that was necessary was a complete Navy communications checkout. A radio network checkout for the Naval communications checkout. A radio network checkout for the Naval communication recovery forces in general. At 10:00 in the evening, the carrier Communications Officer and the Flag Communications Officer both checked out the communications link with the Recovery Room back at the Cape. All was clear too with each of the destroyers and through the normal Navy network which was a reliable method up through the Caribbean Islands and to the States straight to Washington and then down the Coast to the Cape. Everything worked perfectly. The intermediate checkouts took place on about 15 minute intervals up till about midnight. At midnight there was a scheduled check-in for the Admiral and all of his ships with Admiral Hillis back at the Cape, in the Recovery Center. Just about ten minutes prior to midnight the old Admiral came out in his bathrobe, trousers and carpet slippers and asked, "How are things going?" His Operations Officer said, "Oh fine sir, everything is going well." The Admiral checked the charts and our location with relation to the target area and said, "Fine, fine we'll be ready to go." About two minutes to midnight he stationed himself, microphone in hand, ready to check in with the Admiral on the beach. At precisely midnight he said, "Hello, Charlie, this is George. Can you read?" Nothing happened. And he repeated this a half dozen times and nothing happened. Almost one minute after midnight the destroyers started reporting in to the Cape on schedule. Each one of them reported in as planned and everything went like clockwork. Meantime, the Admiral was storming. He said, "I've got over a million dollars worth of communications equipment on this ship and I can't even talk to the beach." The two Communications Officers were scurrying to relieve the frustration and trying to find out what had happened.

Of course, as I mentioned before, during the night we had been driving at full speed to the Champlain's recovery station. We had shaken the radio equipment pretty badly. It was located right above the carrier's heaviest vibration center, and this very likely had knocked out some of the radio gear. They got the thing working within twenty minutes or so and he could talk to the Recovery boss on the beach. Admiral Hillis was happy that we were near the predicted impact point and told us that the count back at Cape was progressing well. The two Communications Officers stood in the shadows on the flag bridge and breathed much easier but I believe that throughout the mission the pressure and stress wore most heavily on these young fellows. It must have aged each of them several years.

A number of aircraft from the carriers in the abort recovery, and the first and second orbit contingency recovery areas came into Bermuda on Business during the "hold" on John's mission. The Navy flight crews stayed at the BOQ where we were billeted. The usual chatter went on in the lobby at the desk and in the sitting room just in side the front door.

One evening I remember one young naval officer was saying, "Well, tomorrow back to the old scow." I commented that I understood that his ship was one of the "most modern of vessels." He said, "Oh yes, we even have special machinery in the onboard laundry that tears the buttons off your shorts and shoots them through your shirts."

The Admiral's Staff was, I'm sure, very much like any Navy staff since John Paul Jones. Lunch and dinner were always excellent and the company was extremely pleasant. Usually some good natured kidding would develop over baseball, on-shore manly pursuits, or minor technical rivalries of the day. Toward the end of the evening meal the Admiral would ask the Flag Lt. "What's the movie this evening?" As if by prearrangement all of the Captains, Commanders and the rest of us would look at the Lt. and with an air of deliberate reluctance the Lt. took a deep breath and said "Sundown At Hard Rock Gulch", Sir." Another western was on its way. The Admiral's liking for western movies no doubt had a sweeping effect on the content of the movie film canisters exchanged among the ships of the A.S.W. team while they plied the Atlantic in pursuit of the National Defense.

Julian Hart of the Los Angeles Herald Tribune representing the daily papers in the press pool aboard the Randolph, met me at the cold drink faucet frequently during the countdown. The Navy crew, as I have said, had provided sandwiches and cold drinks of the Kool-Aid variety -- one purple kind and one orange flavored type. About three a.m. ship board time, we collided cup-in-hand at the same vat. Jules regarded the purple liquid running into my cup and asked, "Marty, are you drinking more these days and enjoying it less?"

The same morning while going forward along one of the passageways below the hangar deck, I spotted a sign on one of the heads, "LADIES" it said. A burley Chief Petty Officer passing in the opposite direction noted my surprise and said, "It's a little nostalgia I guess, sir. That's the one they use when we're in port."

Just prior to the first sight of Gus' arrival in the vicinity of the carrier, Captain Cook called me and said, "We're using a figure eight course pattern crossing through the predicted impact point twice in each pass. How do you feel about landing the capsule on deck?" I said, "Don't do it!! The thing is designed to land in the water, let's land it there and pick it up." He said, "Okay, we'll try to land it along side."

Actually, the area was cloudy and it was obvious we might not be able to see the drogue chute opening as clearly as we saw it at the end of Shepard's flight. So, I left the bridge and climbed to the lookout level on the mast above the main superstructure of the carrier. I watched from here for Gus' arrival listening on the intercom to the incoming reports from the Cape. We could hear the corrected impact point and other data that was coming over the system. About the time the drogue should open and the astronaut had reported that the drogue was open, he was behind the cumulous cloud bank. But very shortly the main chute appeared below the clouds and then we were able to spot the capsule as Gus descended to the blue sea surface. The helicopters had left the carrier, of course, several minutes before and were almost in the area where the impact would occur.

The touchdown went on without incident. You could hear the astronaut talking over the communications links. We could hear the discussion between him and the beach at first and then after touchdown between him and the other communication segments nearby. Almost as soon as he touched down the helicopters were over him. Suddenly, the primary recovery helicopter Marine 44 started a 360 degree turn away from the capsule and so did the secondary recovery helicopter. The Navy helicopters with the photo people aboard moved in over the spacecraft. I jumped out of the crows nest, scampered to the bridge and said, "What happened?" Admiral Clarke told me that the astronaut had asked the helicopter pilots to hold off for a minute till he finished his engineering readings of the instruments on board the spacecraft. This seemed pretty delaying but if he wanted to stay in there for a minute, fine. The sea was fairly calm and with the glasses we could see the spacecraft bobbing gently in the waves. Then all of a sudden there was quite a hubbub out over the area where the capsule was. A brief silence and then Lt. Jim Lewis, who was the Marine pilot of the prime recovery helicopter, reported that he had a positive hookup but that the capsule had shipped a full load of water and that the astronaut was in the water beside the capsule.

From the terse fragmentary comments over the radio it was obvious that Gus had to get out of the capsule in an emergency. The capsule was full of water. The Marine helicopter, No. 44, also had a problem. In fact, they were having difficulty holding the capsule. Then all of a sudden, I got a report that the chopper had a Mayday situation. The helicopter pilot, Lt. Lewis, reported he had a chip signal and had to do something immediately. Should he release the capsule or what? I said, "Drop the capsule and get Gus." He reported that Gus was all right, the secondary recovery chopper was picking Gus up. So they dropped the capsule and headed back to the carrier. At this point we were well within sight although we were not close enough to see exactly what was going on with binoculars.

I turned to the Captain, the Flag Operations Officer and asked to have a buoy marker put over the side to mark the vicinity and assist in locating the sunken spacecraft. He took me to the chart table and pointed to the depth markings on the big sea chart. The number was 1200. I said "1200 feet?" He chuckled and said, "No, 1200 fathoms." Good Lord, the ocean was over five miles deep at that point. We had an adjusted impact point right over the edge of the tremendous cliff which runs approximately north and south under the Atlantic about 200 miles off the coast of Florida.

The helicopter 44 returned to the carrier. The forward deck had been cleared and he landed there. Then the secondary recovery, Marine 41, landed aft near elevator #2, which was designated as the spot where Gus should be put down. They landed as scheduled without problem. The doctors met Gus and took him below.

Meantime I requested the carrier Marine Commander to bring the two Marine crews from the two helicopters to the bridge for a debriefing. Charlie Tynan and I prepared a quick draft teletype report to the beach. We also reported by radio phone to Mr. Williams on the beach.

When the helicopter crews came to the bridge they were visibly and understandably upset and shaken. I got Jim Lewis and told him to relax. Everybody realized he had done what the heck he could do. Gus was all right -- he had come aboard and walked below under his own power. Everything was fine and really, he ought to remember that all of the data of the flight had been telemetered back to the Cape and we had it all. The only things missing were the instruments themselves, and the onboard film. Therefore, there was really no big fat problem and not really a lot to be upset about.

Marine Major joined us and we took Jim and his buddies to the Admiral's quarters behind the flag bridge where they had some coffee and we all sat down. I said, "Now look, we've got to go down to see the press, they are certainly going to be clamoring to talk to you fellows but I want you to talk to them as a group, not separately. Also, the only way to go is to talk to them factually. Tell them exactly what happened as you saw it. This is what Gus is going to have to do when he talks to the press later. As everyone got fairly well calmed down we went down below and aft to the Press Center. Immediately the representatives of the various news media wanted to collar them separately but I announced that they would be interrogated as a group. Stan Miller, Assistant NASA Public Information Director aboard managed the conference. Mr. Mittauer was in the Admiral's quarters as planned along with the doctors and Gus and the ship's executive officer. There wasn't any reasonable way to reach Gus for comment. The ship's marines had very carefully bottled off the area, as prearranged and even I couldn't get in there by my own prior agreement with the Admiral and the Captain of the ship. Therefore, I was probably pretty highhanded, literally taking charge of the public affairs of the thing. However, Stan MIller was there with me and we were later happy to receive the thanks of the radio and TV people as well as McCarey at Fox of the wire service. Shorty Powers also had some good natured kidding and thanks for us too. During the discussion, of course, the whole incident was covered as the crews had seen it. Suddenly they had seen the hatch blow from the capsule and Gus came out through the side almost instantly. It was after they were hooked up so that they were able to keep the capsule up above he water for a bit. Some of the pictures taken from other helicopters indicated the capsule sank to the point where Marine Helicopter No. 44 was down so low that the wheels of the landing gear were in the water.

After we finished the news session I asked the Marines to go immediately to a nearby room where I had arranged for a tape recorder to be ready. There they individually recorded their version of what they had seen during the recovery effort. Later, I returned to the bridge and again called Walt Williams at the Cape and told what had transpired. I also told him that I was arranging for the four Marine pilots to go in a separate air craft from the carrier to the Grand Bahama to be there during Gus' full debriefing. I suggested that they could assist him and the other NASA people in evaluation of the nature of the recovery difficulty and the loss of the capsule. I also told him that I had a tape recording of their comments right after their return to the carrier and that this tape would be with them on the flight from the carrier to the Grand Bahamas.

As previously mentioned, the capsule had sunk in probably the deepest part of the Atlantic. It took with it the onboard film and the instrument records. But the entire collection of scientific data except for the film had been transmitted back to the Cape in real time through the onboard telemetry system. There were evacuated tanks and tanks filled with gas onboard so that the capsule did not sink as a dead weight but retained buoyancy enough so that it probably descended most of the way to the bottom of the crevasse and then settled at some level in a floating condition and remains to drift at two, three, or four miles depth "till the ocean runs dry." In the months to come we were to receive several hundred proposals of methods to recover it. Many of the serious undertakings by reputable firms or individuals, and many of them from crackpots.

The more serious proposals were from a real wide range of people from college professors to prominent aircraft industrial firms. However, the decision on whether to try to recover the spacecraft or not, was based on the fact that the main value of the flight had really been contained in the telemetered data which the Cape receivers had recorded as the flight took place; the hardware was really only of historical value and it was, to Project Mercury at least, not "worth it" to try to get the space capsule back. Important to note of course was that we had plenty of capsules but only one Gus.

There is one account of an occasion when Gus was to make a trip from Orlando and we got word that reporters were waiting for him. He had decided he didn't want to talk anymore about how the capsule sank. So he rounded up a pair of dark glasses and a straw hat for a disguise. He tried them out on Deke and asked, "How do I look?" Slayton told him that he looked just like Gus Grissom in dark glasses and a kookie hat.

I know what happened inside the capsule. Gus is a trained specialist, a Research Test Pilot. He does things while he is flying by a set of pre-agreed... (unfinished thought)

Gus said that after he had been selected to be among the original seven astronauts he used to lie awake at night sometimes and think about the capsule sitting up on top of the giant booster and ask himself, "Now what in hell do you want to get up on that thing for?" He did get up there and ride out over the Atlantic 200 miles atop the roaring, flaming Redstone rocket. He evidently is sold on the mode of transportation because he is all set now to mount the Titan II service tower and take a seat in the Gemini spacecraft with John Young and go for the test mission in orbit before his return to another ocean landing.

I once asked him while we were on duty together at Bermuda during John Glenn's flight whether it was rough to go out to the pad to "mount-up" on the morning of the MR-4 flight.

He said, "You know old Bill Douglas asked me that morning if I was really ready. If I had wanted to call it off there could be a dozen medical reasons he could give for refusing to let me fly ---- You know when you think of all the preparation for the flight, all the guys who had been working all night on the count down, the Navy out at sea waiting, the big national build up on TV, radio and in the press, to say nothing of the cost of it all ---- It would have taken more guts not to go than to go."

Made in the USA
San Bernardino, CA
17 December 2014